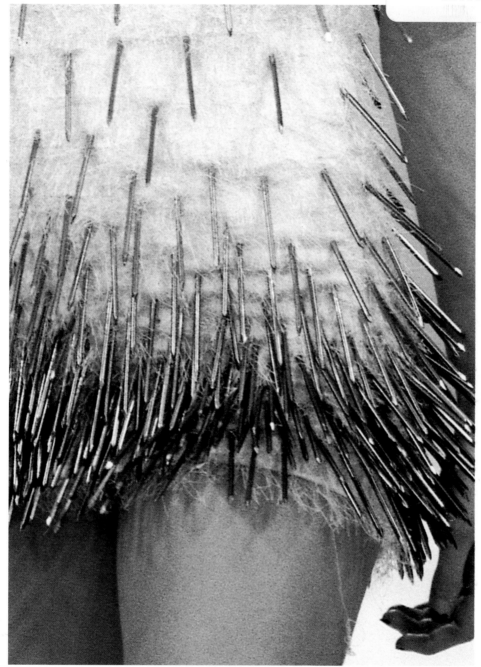

Sue Jenkyn Jones

# Fashion design

Laurence King Publishing

**LAURENCE KING**

Copyright © 2002 Developments at London
Institute Limited. Published in 2002 by
Laurence King Publishing Ltd in association
with Central Saint Martins

Laurence King Publishing Ltd
71 Great Russell Street, London WC1B 3BP
T: +44 20 7430 8850  F: +44 20 7430 8880
E: enquiries@laurenceking.co.uk
www.laurenceking.co.uk

A catalogue record for this book is available from
the British Library.

ISBN 1 85669 245 0

Designed by Christopher Wilson

Printed in China

*Cover*  Dress by Elin Hagberg and James Norris,
photograph by Honey Salvadori
*Frontispiece*  Dress by Andrew Groves,
photograph by Niall McInerney

# Introduction

Womenswear

# Who this book is for

The media has perpetuated the myth that fashion professionals lead a glamorous and carefree existence. They are shown living in beautiful homes or hobnobbing at parties and weddings with the wealthy and the famous. Only a small proportion of fashion professionals – the most talented and the luckiest – live like this, and most will have worked tremendously hard to achieve their apparent 'overnight' success. The majority of fashion designers are never famous or rich and work happily enough behind the scenes in satisfying jobs for more or less ordinary wages. Becoming a fashion professional is not a soft option, and the demands are considerable – creatively, personally, intellectually, technically and even physically. Yet it can be a joy to find that you are actually getting paid for doing what you love best.

> 'Designers have to play many parts – artist, scientist, psychologist, politician, mathematician, economist, salesman – combined with the stamina of the long-distance runner.' Designer Helen Storey

Fashion design is one of the most oversubscribed subjects in higher education. Fashion is such a popular career choice that very few people succeed in it without thorough preparation. With only a handful of apprentice-level openings in tailoring and *haute couture*, it is difficult to enter the industry without at least a first degree. Higher-education courses aim to teach and nurture the skills required in the market place. While they cannot guarantee success, they offer thorough and compatible training. Moreover, their links with industry and established designers make them highly useful for a student's future career.

This book will be of use primarily to the aspiring student, but it should also appeal to the fashion enthusiast. It attempts to give a balanced insider view of fashion education and to explain the talents, skills, specialisms and techniques that could qualify a student to work in the fashion industry. The majority of fashion books are cultural histories, biographies of individual designers or technical manuals, and there is little to explain the training, the industry or the process of turning the creative impulse into a product. This book shows how the designer can become skilled at reading the prevailing aesthetic, altering it and applying the synthesized result to the body in a desirable and marketable way. Because fashion is a service industry, where creativity takes place against a backdrop of different tastes and market sectors, global trading and growing technological complexity, this book also explores the differences between markets and manufacturing styles, traditional methodology and newfangled processes. This book will serve as a guide to these areas and the range of job opportunities available.

While *Fashion Design* touches on many aspects of its subject, it can only provide an overview; the more technical and advanced facets of pattern-construction, dressmaking and tailoring are not included. Many of these techniques require hands-on practice and cannot be fully learnt from a book. There are no projects for the reader but many suggestions for self-reflection, further reading and investigation. This book will not give advice on how to dress well or forecast the future of fashion, but for anyone who is committed to a career in the fashion industry it will give an insight into how others have reached their goals.

The examples of teaching and learning styles, project briefs and pathways are not offered prescriptively. It is my experience that every student group is different, both in terms of its personality and its response to the world it encounters. The same projects can yield entirely different results in different hands and at different times. One of the great pleasures of being a student is the experience of sharing and learning from the surprises, triumphs and mistakes of others.

# How to use the book

*Fashion Design* is both a manual and a careers guide. It attempts to give a comprehensive flavour of fashion design as an international market and global operation. It aims to inform, inspire and guide, often by using the testimonies of those who have already travelled the route, walked the walk and talked the talk. Although some of the information may be stated as fact, there is no right or wrong way to become a fashion professional or achieve an effective fashion solution. Fashion people are often rebels who know that rules are made to be broken.

The fashion-degree curriculum typically set outs to familiarize students with increasingly complex practical and intellectual demands and simulates many of the tasks and sequences that the real-life designer needs to master. In this book, the range of information and concepts that a student is likely to encounter is set out across seven chapters, which can be dipped into and consulted in any order.

Chapter I, 'Context', sets out the historical and contemporary settings against which fashion designers position their wares. It describes the fundamental requirements of clothing and the way that fashion choices can cut irrationally across them. It shows how both commercial considerations and an ability to tune in to current needs, trends and underlying social preoccupations guide the designer's inspiration. This chapter also introduces the fashion world and important centres for design and manufacturing. The structure of the industry itself, including facts and figures, market sectors, **price points** and the revolving **fashion cycle** are explained in Chapter II, 'From manufacture to market'.

Chapter III, 'The body', explores the primary impulse for creativity in fashion and shows how the shape, movement and behaviour of the human body inform and impact on fashion design. Physical types and the prevailing aesthetic are discussed, and the use of proportion and design principles in relation to the form is explained. Drawing and illustrating the body and clothing are skills central to the practice of fashion design, and the different styles and approaches to illustration and industry requirements are shown by example. The chapter also highlights how the industry uses the computer, both for illustration and presentation of artwork and for creative research and promotion.

Chapter IV, 'Colour and fabric', explores the most stimulating and fascinating variables in the designer's tool kit. Chapter V, 'In the studio', takes the reader into the design studio and introduces the practical processes of design, from the pattern-cutting table to the finished garment. People have been making clothes by these means for centuries, but fashion and its techniques renew themselves constantly.

Chapter VI, 'The brief', takes the reader through the staple of fashion degree courses: the setting of the project brief. It explores how a student should interpret and respond to the brief. It explains how to go about researching and finding

Menswear

information and how to synthesize the result into original fashion ideas. It shows how the daunting process of the project **crit** can be an exciting and productive experience that hones students' critical awareness and presentation skills as well as preparing them for work on their degree collection and the final fashion show.

The last chapter, 'The final collection – and beyond', is about leaving the fashion course as a newly fledged designer and the search for employment. Where can a student's talents be put to best use? How does he or she go about finding those elusive jobs? Jobs may not be easy to land, but this chapter helps students to prepare for the outside world by explaining the importance of the **portfolio** and the curriculum vitae (CV), or résumé, and by outlining the interviewing procedure.

At the end of the book there are guides to further reading, address lists for suppliers, organizations and places of research, and a glossary of terms. Like any other industry, fashion has a lot of jargon, and a mastery of it will go some way in opening up some of its apparent mysteries. Throughout this book the use of bold type indicates that an explanation of the word or words can be found in the glossary.

# Have you got what it takes?

Before launching yourself on what may be a long and arduous path to a career in the fashion industry, it pays to try and find out whether you have the right qualities and have a realistic idea of your own strengths and weaknesses. Below is an alphabetical checklist of the desirable personal qualities and skills you will need to demonstrate in order to enter the field. Evaluating yourself on a scale of one to five will help you to gauge your aptitudes. Discuss your score with a friend or teacher to see where your talents and shortcomings lie.

**Checklist of personal qualities and skills**

*Ambition* A strong will to achieve – practically, conceptually and financially.
*Artistic – 2-D skills* An ability to visualize, draw and paint in two dimensions.
*Artistic – 3-D skills* An ability to make up ideas in three dimensions using materials.
*Assertiveness* Stating your point of view clearly; standing by your beliefs.
*Charm* Getting on well with others; good communication; the ability to cooperate.
*Colour sense* Important for range-building, print, childrenswear and knitwear.
*Commitment* Hard-working, open to learning, prepared to 'go the extra mile'.
*Communication skills* Delegating, explaining, listening and negotiating; speaking to groups.
*Confidence* Faith in your ideas and skills and in those of others; keeping a good balance between egotism and humility.
*Conscientiousness* Thoroughness, diligence, 'taking the rough with the smooth'.
*Creativity* Innate talent combined with an ability to learn to generate and analyse ideas.
*Curiosity* Interest in society, people, design, function and form, etc; being well-informed.
*Decisiveness* Making decisions and taking responsibility for moving forward.
*Efficiency* Time-planning and organization of information and materials; meeting deadlines.
*Energy* Physical stamina, health and the ability to stick to the job at hand.

Talent and creativity

*Flair* Making hard work seem effortless; good grooming, sense of style.

*Flexibility* Adaptability and embracing others' criticism; accepting change.

*Humility* The ability to ask for help; knowing your place in the hierarchy.

*Imagination* Creativity and well-tuned inspiration.

*Independence* – of thought, not behaviour; an ability to work unsupervised or freelance.

*Initiative* Introducing new ideas, starting projects.

*Passion* An enthusiasm for fashion; involvement; the ability to inspire others.

*Patience* Seeing things through; tolerance for repetitive tasks; 'suffering fools gladly'.

*Perception* A quick eye; intellectual and graphic skills; troubleshooting.

*Practical skills* – can be learned but should be appropriate for the task; wide-ranging.

*Resourcefulness* Ingenuity, lateral thinking, problem-solving; 'making do'.

*Risk-taking* Daring; 'chutzpah', foresight, entrepreneurial skills.

*Temperament* Calm, with the ability to cope and remain cheerful and stress-free.

*Writing skills* An ability to communicate on paper and write reports.

Above all, you need talent. A talent for fashion design is not necessarily the same as a talent for drawing, nor is it the ability to sew, although it does include both of these. Fashion design goes far beyond this, and what will be expected of you is the ability to research, absorb and synthesize ideas and skills. Fashion creativity is the ability to produce new variants and solutions to the age-old problem of clothing the body and refreshing and exciting awareness of it in a contemporary context.

'The trick is to give people what they never knew they wanted.'
Diana Vreeland, editor of American *Vogue* from 1963 to 1971

After your training you may need to develop new qualities and skills. The following are additional attributes that the workplace may demand of you:

Ability to live on a shoestring

Accuracy of designs or records

Authority over others

Computer design skills

Connections

Diplomacy

Discretion

Driving licence

Fitting into an environment or culture

Financial acuity

Languages

Loyalty

Memory for names and details

Modest expectations

Numeracy

Prestige

Punctuality

Reliability and good health

Socializing after hours

Sense of humour

Speed

Teamwork

Travel

Willingness to work long hours and at weekends

# The first steps

If these two lists have not left you daunted, and you still believe that a career in fashion is for you – go for it! Start by collecting college prospectuses and brochures to help you choose where you would like to study. Colleges put on an exhibition of their graduating students' work at the end of the final term. For fashion courses there is usually a catwalk show and also an exhibition of portfolio work, sometimes held independently of each other. Contact the college office to enquire. Don't be daunted by the standard of final-year work; this is what you should aspire to, not what would be expected of you in your first year. By visiting the degree shows you will get some idea of the range of pathways open to you and the quality of the course and its range of resources. It's worth asking the students, too, about their own experiences of the course.

**Which college?**

The aim of all fashion courses is to make the training as relevant as possible to finding work in the industry. However, colleges vary quite considerably in their focus and approach and in their facilities. Some are better equipped with machinery and technology; others have inspiring and skilled staff. A good balance of all these factors is desirable but not inevitable.

Nowadays, colleges often offer both full-time and part-time courses. Sandwich courses require students to spend a period in a work-experience programme or industrial placement. There are also internationally recognized credit schemes that allow students to pursue a period of study at another institute or university or in another country. Some courses are biased towards technology, while others emphasize practical skills. Some will be combination degrees that include business or cultural studies. The time allotted to studio practice and self-directed learning or attendance will vary enormously, as will the length of time required to take the qualification itself.

Colleges are keen to show prospective students their facilities and exhibit their strengths. Open days for this purpose are usually held well before the application forms need to be sent in. It is important not to rely solely on the prospectus or word of mouth when choosing a college. Location, atmosphere and infrastructure will all be become much clearer during a visit, and visitors are likely to be given access to parts of the campus that are normally out of bounds at other times. Moreover, college tutors will not be impressed if a candidate turns up for interview without having visited previously – unless, of course, you live overseas.

Fabric design

## Which course?

College prospectuses list a bewildering range of courses. Unless you have grown up with a burning desire to be a hosiery designer or milliner, it is very hard to pick your way through the minefield of possibilities. Don't worry: colleges assume that you may make a mistake and will want to change options later, although it does help if you can narrow the field beforehand. Before applying for any course, you should investigate the level of qualification, curriculum, methods of study and the subject pathways or options available. Many colleges will expect you to define your chosen pathway on the application form. Others will run a diagnostic programme that will help you to find your areas of aptitude during your first, or freshman, year.

The most popular choice of pathway for students is womenswear design. Many courses focus almost exclusively on this area, and currently seven times as many people apply for training in this field than in any other. Womenswear, however, has long had a reputation for being the most fickle sector of the clothing industry, with the greatest and fastest turnover of jobs. It may be useful to visit a large department store and work your way around from floor to floor, assessing the merchandise. Go from the 'madame' department to the trendy concessions and ask yourself not what *you* like to buy or wear, but which sector of the market interests you from the designing, fabrication and customer points of view. If it is not one of these markets, perhaps it is streetwear or extreme sportswear. All are valid areas in the study of fashion.

Broadly, the subjects on offer are Fashion Design Womenswear; Fashion Design Menswear; Fashion Design with Marketing; Fashion Design with Print; Fashion Design with Knitwear; and Fashion Communication and Promotion. Fashion with Business Studies or Merchandising are also commonly offered. A few colleges also offer childrenswear, lingerie, sportswear, or shoes and accessories as options. You may be able to choose only one pathway or you may be able to mix and match a number.

Knitwear

## Application procedures

The procedures required when applying to a college vary considerably. In addition to listing academic qualifications and experience, the application form normally requires applicants to write a brief piece about themselves, their interests and achievements and their reasons for wishing to join the course. It is worth writing a draft version first. Try to write as succinctly as possible and avoid clichés; check spellings carefully – especially the names of designers who have inspired you – and have someone read over your effort and give an opinion before you commit it to the form. Keep a copy and refer to it before your interview, as you will probably be asked questions based on what you have written. You may be asked to supply a confidential reference or testimony.

Most art college courses will require you to show a portfolio for assessment, usually at an interview. Interviewing differs from college to college, especially in the time given to each candidate. In a few cases you may not actually be seen, but your portfolio will be reviewed by an expert team of staff. It is therefore very important that you have an idea of the amount and kinds of work you should submit in your portfolio (see below). Most college applicants have built up a strong portfolio on a foundation or other pre-college programme such as a BTEC course.

Some colleges offer short courses on portfolio presentation; tutors on these programmes will help you define and refine your area of interest and show you how to edit your portfolio.

### The interview portfolio

At an interview for a college place at foundation or first-degree level, your examiners will be looking for a wide range of artistic abilities rather than a very narrowly focused interest in fashion alone. You will be expected to have made some life studies from actual observation, showing an awareness of the body as a three-dimensional form, as well as rapid line drawings that suggest its fluidity and movement. Colour studies (but not college exercises) and paintings and drawings that show your confidence and control over a wide range of media will also be helpful.

Sketchbooks showing your visual research and ideas and experiments in progress will stand you in good stead. Demonstrate a feeling for fabric by keeping clippings and ideas for their use in a sketchbook. Fashion drawings are expected but not essential. Never copy from other sources or published photographs; use your own drawing skills, even if they are undeveloped, and try to show a good sense of line and proportion. If you have done three-dimensional work or sculptures, show photographs of them rather than bringing them with you. Similarly, if you have made garments there is unlikely to be time to show or model them. At this point, teaching staff will not be interested primarily in your technical expertise but in your ideas.

Organize the work so that it is easy to go through, as a series of projects or in order of impact rather than chronology. You don't have to mount, frame or finish work; this can make it look too precious or heavy. Put charcoal and pastel drawings in plastic sleeves or paper to prevent smearing. Know your way around your portfolio; you will probably be asked to point out a favourite piece of work or explain some aspect of a project. Be prepared to talk about your own design processes and show how you arrived at a solution.

In Chapter VII there is a section on how to put together a professional portfolio which you might find helpful. However, be aware that at this early stage in your career the interviewers are looking for your raw potential and not a slick, 'know-it-all' presentation.

# The college syllabus

The content of a syllabus will vary according to the programme of study and the particular needs and interests of the students. Time given to different subjects will vary, too, and tutors will bring their individual expertise to bear on the course. A comprehensive fashion-design syllabus aims to deliver the following:

Awareness of contemporary fashion and visual culture
Basic principles of pattern-cutting and draping fabric
Computer-aided design (CAD)
Design development
Drawing and illustration
Fabric awareness: type, performance and sourcing
Fashion basics: silhouette, proportion, colour, detailing and fabric manipulation

Garment construction and technology
Independent study
Marketing and business awareness
Presentation (portfolio) and communication techniques
Range-building
Research techniques and methods
Technical specification and costing
Written work, as in report-writing and cultural studies

Typically, fashion degrees last three years (although courses of two and four years also exist), each year being divided into three terms or two semesters.

### The first year

During the first year, projects are often short and diverse so as to give students a broad, basic grounding in the various fashion-related areas. The greatest attention is given to stretching students' abilities to assimilate information and tackle research – which can later be turned into original design work. Some time is devoted to practical assignments to improve skills, confidence and speed. The results of the project work are put together in a portfolio, which over the years builds into a professional representation of a student's ability and style.

### The second year

By the second year, students are likely to have a greater sense of direction and will have gained confidence in their abilities. Usually they will have learned the basic skills and how to negotiate with staff and fellow students. This is a year for consolidating abilities, with the focus on getting the balance right between teamwork and the evolution of an individual style. Projects will usually be of four to six weeks' duration and will help refine students' interests and talents within their chosen course of study.

Second-year students often make more ambitious garments and enter competitions and sponsored projects. At this stage students often work in teams or pairs in order to hone their cooperative and interpersonal skills. They are less closely supervised in the hope that they will reach the level of maturity and self-discipline required to progress to the next stage of the course.

'If you wanted to, you could do nothing – but why?' Second-year student

### Work experience: the internship

At some point in the course – usually between the second and third years – some fashion courses offer an industrial placement or work-experience period of varied or negotiable length. This is an opportunity to work in the industry: in design studios, production or promotion, at home or possibly overseas. At this juncture the student should have enough practical skills and commitment to be useful as a junior employee, as well as enough maturity to use the opportunity to evaluate his or her own qualities and ambitions within a real working environment.

If a student works for a company long enough, he or she may experience the full cycle of a collection, from initial idea to public reception. This can be an enjoy-able and salutary lesson. The student may be exposed to aspects of fashion and production that are new and inspiring or that uncover previously untapped talents.

Casualwear

The internship is a period of study, not time out, and students are usually asked to produce a written report on their placements, including a critical analysis of the organization for which they worked. It is worth remembering that the fashion industry is very keen to take on graduates who have prior experience of the workplace, and that a placement can lead to a lasting association – or can at least be a source of useful contacts.

'I went to India. I met lots of craftsmen and was able to realize the potential of working with embroidery.' Designer Matthew Williamson

**Final year**

'When I was at college I did a lot of designing on paper and not much making. You don't get time to make things properly in the first and second year. I found it very frustrating just working with illustration. In the final year it all comes together and you can see the results of what you have been learning. I really liked that.' Designer Suzanne Clements

During the final year the projects are more intensive, giving students time to explore the ideas in depth and to perfect their techniques. The year ends with the most important and exciting project brief of all: the final collection (see page 161). This is the students' opportunity to refine their interests and allow their self-expression, style and proficiency to blossom. Students are asked to design a range of between six and ten outfits appropriate to their specialist study. The final collection should prove that a student can maintain a sustained involvement in the management and resolution of his or her work and is able to design independently and to a professional standard.

At the end of this process, students have the opportunity to show their outfits to the examination board, to staff, fellow students and an invited audience (including industry professionals) at a catwalk show. Their portfolios may also be exhibited to the public – press, sponsors and many interested manufacturers attend degree shows in order to find employees. A student should now be ready to leave the nest as a fully-fledged fashion designer.

# Context I

# The uses of clothing

Fashion is a specialized form of body adornment. Explorers and travellers were among the first to document and comment on the body adornment and dress styles that they encountered around the world. Some returned from their travels with drawings and examples of clothing, sparking off a desire not only for the artefacts themselves but also for an understanding of them. Eventually the study of clothing came to be an accepted part of anthropology – the scientific study of human beings.

Cultural theorists and clothing analysts have since focused primarily on four practical functions of dress: utility, modesty, immodesty (that is, sexual attraction) and adornment. In his book *Consumer Behaviour Towards Dress* (1979), George Sproles suggested four additional functions: symbolic differentiation, social affiliation, psychological self-enhancement and modernism. Each of these eight functions is discussed briefly below.

## Utility

Clothing has evolved to meet many practical and protective purposes. The environment is hazardous, and the body needs to be kept at a mean temperature to ensure blood circulation and comfort. The bushman needs to keep cool, the fisherman to stay dry; the firemen needs protection from flames and the miner from harmful gases. Dress reformers have typically put utility above other aesthetic considerations. For example, in the 1850s the American publisher and suffrage pioneer Amelia Jenks Bloomer took issue with the impracticality of the crinoline and advocated the wearing of women's trousers, called 'pantalettes' or 'bloomers'. The notion of utility should never be underestimated; consumers often chose clothes with concerns such as comfort, durability or ease of care in mind. In recent years, fitness clothing and sportswear – themselves originally utility items – have dominated the leisure-clothing markets and become fashionable as indicators of health and youthful stamina.

**Opposite** Fashion has been infused with the healthy allure of sports clothing.

**Above** Utility: besides wearing heavy protective equipment, a coal mine rescue worker also carried a caged linnet as a safety alarm.

**Below left** Fashion students in 1897 investigate clothing engravings in the Bibliothèque Nationale, Paris.

**Modesty and Immodesty**

**Top** In parts of the Middle East, strict laws still forbid women to reveal any part of their bodies.

**Above** The shifting erogenous zone: in the 1920s the legs and the back were the focus of attention, enhanced by dance crazes such as the Charleston and the Tango.

**Above right** By contrast, in Western society this type of beachwear would now be considered absurd and antiquated.

## Modesty

We need clothing to cover our nakedness. Society demands propriety and has often passed sumptuary (clothing) laws to curb extravagance and uphold decorum. Most people feel some insecurity about revealing their physical imperfections, especially as they grow older; clothing disguises and conceals our defects, whether real or imagined. Modesty is socially defined and varies among individuals, groups and societies, as well as over time.

## Immodesty (Sexual attraction)

Clothing can be used to accentuate the sexual attractiveness and availability of the wearer. Woman's traditional role as a passive sexual object has contributed to the greater eroticization of female clothing. Evening wear and lingerie are made from fabrics that set off or simulate the texture of skin. Accessories and cosmetics are also used to enhance allure. Many fashion commentators and theorists have used

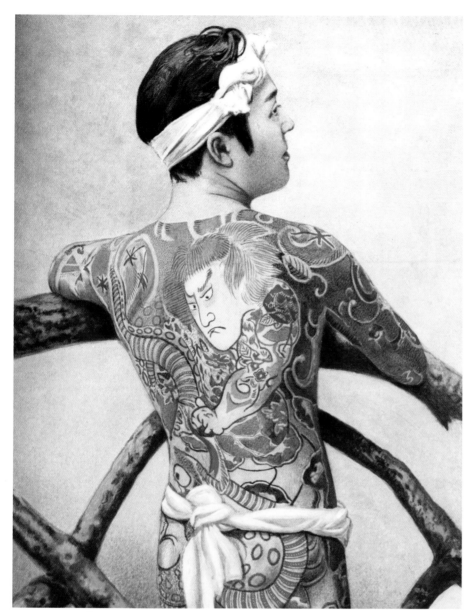

a psychoanalytic approach, based on the writings of Sigmund Freud and Carl Jung, to explain the unconscious processes underlying changes in fashion.

## Adornment

Adornment allows us to enrich our physical attractions, assert our creativity and individuality, or signal membership or rank within a group or culture. Adornment can go against the needs for comfort, movement and health, as in foot-binding, the wearing of corsets, or piercing and tattooing. Adornments can be permanent or temporary, additions to or reductions of the human body. Cosmetics and body paint, jewellery, hairstyling and shaving, false nails, wigs and hair extensions, suntans, high heels and plastic surgery are all body adornments. People generally, and young women in particular, attempt to conform to the prevailing ideal of beauty. Bodily contortions and reshaping through foundation garments, padding and binding have altered the fashionable silhouette throughout the ages.

**Adornment**
**Above left** The tattoo is a permanent corporal adornment.

**Above right** A girl from the Yemen is decorated with flowers and ornaments on her wedding day.

## Symbolic differentiation

People use clothing to differentiate and recognize profession, religious affiliation, social standing or lifestyle. Occupational dress is an expression of authority and helps the wearer stand out in a crowd. The modest attire of a nun announces her beliefs. In some countries, lawyers and barristers cover their everyday clothes with the garb of silk and periwig in order to convey the solemnity of the law. The wearing of designer labels or insignia and expensive materials and jewellery may start as items of social distinction, but often trickle down through the social strata until they lose their potency as symbols of differentiation.

## Social affiliation

People dress alike in order to belong to a group. Those who do not conform to the accepted styles are assumed to have divergent ideas and are ultimately mistrusted and excluded. Conversely, the fashion victim, who conforms without sensitivity to the rules of current style, is perceived as being desperate to belong and lacking in personality and taste. In some cases clothing is a statement of rebellion against society or fashion itself. Although punks do not have a uniform, they can be recognized by a range of identifiers: torn clothes, bondage items, safety pins, dramatic hairstyles and so on. This dress code was developed by the British fashion designer Vivienne Westwood as an anarchic jibe against the conventional, well-groomed fashions of the mid-1970s.

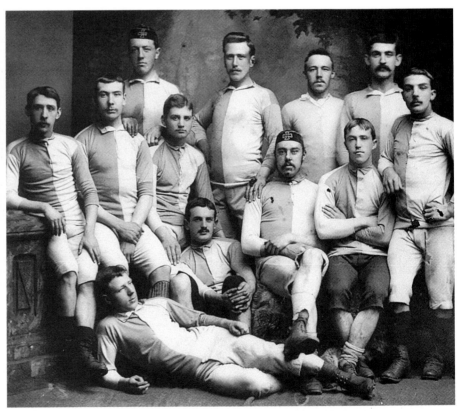

### Symbolic differentiation

**Top** The coronation gowns of King George V and Queen Mary denote authority and status through their weight and the expense of the materials used.

**Above** At the other end of the social scale, a Pearly Queen marks her position in the community by emulating the regal robes and embroideries in buttons.

### Social affiliation

**Above** The soccer team and its supporters dress alike in order to demonstrate their allegiance and conformity.

### Psychological self-enhancement

**Opposite** Dress codes exist at all levels of society. The Doctor Marten boot and frayed jeans were ubiquitous rebel youth-wear throughout the 1970s and 1980s.

## Psychological self-enhancement

Although there is social pressure to be affiliated to a group, and many identical garments and fashions are manufactured and sold through vast chain stores, we rarely encounter two people dressed identically from head to toe. While many young people shop with friends to help and advise each other, they do not buy the same outfits. Whatever the situation, individuals will strive to assert their own personal identity through the use of make-up, hairstyling and accessories.

## Modernism

In parts of the world where fashionable clothes are widely available, dress can be used to express modernity. In the media-rich environment of capital cities, being seen to be ahead or abreast of new styles and aware of current events can give us the edge in an increasingly competitive employment marketplace. The right clothing can grant us access to the right places and the right people. Our acceptance of modernity, whether as designers, early adopters or consumers, serves as an indicator of our creativity, adjustment and preparation for the future.

> 'All fashion is clothing, although clearly not all clothing is fashion …
> We need fashion, rather than clothes, not to clothe our nakedness but to
> clothe our self-esteem.' Colin McDowell (1995)

# The language of fashion

A study of fashion history and of the costumes and customs of different countries will reveal that all societies, from the most primitive to the most sophisticated, use clothing and adornments to communicate social and personal information. Just as we attempt to read the facial expressions of those around us, we also read the signals given by their clothing and draw inferences, sometimes mistakenly, about the kind of people they are. This non-verbal communication – the language of fashion – can be learned like any other language (see opposite).

Throughout history many items and styles of clothing have taken on symbolic meaning, so facilitating the identification of strangers. In his book, *The Fashion System* (1967), the French critic Roland Barthes wrote on the symbolic language of clothes and the way that they inform our socio-political orientation. The study of the signs and symbols that communicate information is called semiotics.

We buy clothes and wear them in combinations that are deliberately or sub-consciously contrived to convey either true or false impressions of ourselves to others. Some of the personal characteristics that we wish to reveal or hide include our age, sexual orientation, size, shape, economic or marital status, occupation, religious affiliation, self-esteem, attitudes and importance. In theatre and film, costume designers actively manipulate the symbolic meaning of clothing by loading the characters with items that we recognize as typical of various occupations and attitudes. A wide range of stereotypes has evolved in this way.

It is the job of fashion designers to experiment with identity and appearances through dress. They must offer clothing that allows people the opportunity to project their own fantasies, be it pop star or princess. In recent years designers have also been challenging the traditional messages communicated by clothing. The diversity of ethnic and subcultural styles has led to distortions of the codes: for example, cardigans worn with saris or tweed jackets worn with jeans. Fashion designers have borrowed from the semiotics of clothes and pushed the boundaries by intentionally destroying principles and harmonies of clothing through oversizing, using clashing colours, designing without reference to body contours, creating sexual ambiguity, using juxtapositions of unusual fabrics and deliberately poor or exposed finishes. For the fashion historian, journalist and anthropologist, learning, interpreting and adding to this creative lexicon is of vital interest.

**Right** Leather, tattoos and chains are stereo-typical garb for the rebel or rocker.

**Opposite** The wearing of fur and jewellery continues to indicate wealth, but it can also express vulgarity.

**Messages traditionally communicated by twentieth-century Western clothing**

| | |
|---|---|
| *Masculinity* | Trousers, ties, broad shoulders, rough or heavy fabrics, outdoor clothing. |
| *Femininity* | Skirts, low necklines, defined waists, delicate fabrics. |
| *Sexual maturity* | Tight clothing, transparent or shiny fabrics, high heels. |
| *Immaturity* | Shapeless, loose clothes, dungarees, childish prints or patterns, bright colours, flat shoes. |
| *Dominance* | Uniforms, uncomfortable fabrics, oversized shoulders, dark colours, leather, metal buttons, large hats and accessories. |
| *Submissiveness* | Impractical fabrics and frills, pale colours, decorative shoes. |
| *Intelligence* | Reading glasses, blue or dark stockings, sombre colours, briefcase. |
| *Conformity* | Dull, chain-store clothing, pressed creases, low-key colours. |
| *Rebellion* | Extreme clothing and hairstyles, tattoos, piercing, unusual shoes or no shoes at all. |
| *Occupation* | Uniforms, suits, wearing of tools and trade accessories. |
| *Origin* | Indicated by town or country clothes or regional dress. |
| *Wealth* | Gold jewellery and gems, clean or new clothes, perfect fit, identifiable fashion labels, dramatic colour, fur, perfume. |
| *Health* | Casual or sporty clothing and logos, body-revealing cut, slim figure, trainers (sneakers). |
| *Age* | Adherence to past styles. |

**Above** A Charles Frederick Worth gown from 1875.

**Opposite** The House of Givenchy, Paris.

# The geography of fashion

Today fashion is a global enterprise. Clothing and fashions are designed and produced in most of the large metropolitan centres. In addition, thriving textile industries in the Far East have encouraged the growth of domestic fashion industries. Fashion designers are trained in many different places, and it is now the norm for designers and fashion workers to move about from one fashion capital to another. Household names such as Chanel, Donna Karan and Calvin Klein, many of which are owned by international conglomerates, have the financial clout and cachet to sell into hitherto untapped markets. In large cities from Seoul to Rio de Janeiro people dress in a Western manner and there is a sizeable and sophisticated market for designer products. Travel and the transportation of goods have become cheaper and more efficient. New technology and satellite communications have sped up the transmission of orders and payments. News and trends travel as fast as the speed of light, thanks to the fax machine and the internet. On one level, fashion is about making money in any currency as fast as possible.

Although the fashion world is constantly growing and dispersing, the French capital, Paris, still retains its traditional dominance. It is still the case that only 'the designer who has made it in Paris has really made it' (Holly Brubach, *New York Times*, 1989). The reason for this goes back to the nineteenth century, when, in 1858, the Englishman Charles Frederick Worth, who is generally thought of as the first couturier, founded a design house in Paris – at that time the cultural and artistic capital of Europe, if not of the world. Because of the popularity of his gowns, which were worn by such illustrious women as Queen Victoria and the Empress Eugènie, Worth's creations fell prey to counterfeiters. To protect his designs he founded the Federation of Parisian Tailors in 1868. The body was responsible for the marketing and manufacturing of fashion and in time grew into the organization now called La Fédération Française de la Couture du Prêt-à-porter des Couturiers et des Créateurs de la Mode. In 1975 a section dealing with *prêt-à-porter* (ready-to-wear clothing) was added. The federation operates three Chambre Syndicales: the Chambre Sydicale de la Couture Parisienne, the Chambre Syndicale du Prêt-à-Porter des Couturiers et des Créateurs de Mode and the Chambre Syndicale de la Mode Masculine. There are stringent rules for qualification and acceptance of membership of the federation; the business must have an atelier or salon in Paris, employ at least twenty full-time staff and stage two collection showings of at least seventy-five outfits twice a year, during the spring and autumn.

The French government has always been very supportive of the needle trades, and French design firms and supporting industries are mutually cooperative and willing to experiment. French television is government-owned and gives French fashion free exposure to help generate home and export sales. The government also offers subsidies to couturiers who use more than 90 per cent French fabrics in their collections. Because it is comparatively easy for designers to achieve their creative ambitions in Paris, the French capital has become internationally central to the industry. Many British, Japanese and European designers now show their ranges there and have moved their main fashion offices and salons to Paris. In 1989 the French government provided seven million francs to build a salon for the showing of collections at the Louvre, encompassing four halls and seating for 4,000 people.

# Two kinds of fashion

There are two main approaches to garment design and production. These are *haute couture* (from the French for 'high tailoring'), where the garments are individually measured, cut and custom-made or custom-designed for clients, and *prêt-à-porter* (French for 'ready-to-wear'), where the garments are made in bulk, to standard sizes and for a target market.

### *Haute couture*

Haute couture is the top end of the market, built on the prestige and success of made-to-measure, hand-stitched, one-off outfits sold to the affluent and socially mobile. Notable couture houses active today are Valentino, Versace, Chanel, Dior, Lacroix, Givenchy, Balmain, Balenciaga, Lanvin and Yves Saint Laurent.

Originally, couture design was by its very nature a slowly evolving, customer-centred form of fashion. However, after the revolutionary 'New Look' created by Christian Dior in 1947, collections were increasingly made without regard to individuals' wishes but rather following the vision of the designer. Later, during the 1960s, designers such as Pierre Cardin, André Courrèges and Paco Rabanne pioneered the idea of *haute couture* as experimental, artistic fashion. Because of the very high prices it commanded, this kind of *haute couture* gradually lost ground to boutique fashion designers such as Mary Quant and American designers such as Rudi Gernreich and Ralph Lauren.

**Right** A private showing for couture clients at the House of Balmain, Paris (1953).

**Opposite** The trouser suit was popularized by Mary Quant in 1960s' London. A demand for cheap and fashionable clothes led to a proliferation of boutiques and independent shops (1967).

Nowadays, the wearing of *haute couture* is no longer so appropriate or so lucrative; prices are prohibitive and the core clientele is estimated to consist of just 2,000 women, the majority of whom are wealthy, elderly Americans. Many of the couture houses form part of the stable of powerful conglomerates such as LVMH (Louis Vuitton, Moët Hennessy). Ownership of these luxury labels changes hands for vast sums of money, often without the knowledge of the general public, but in recent years there have been frequent ugly takeover battles and lawsuits. The collections are used as glamorous advertisements for other products owned by the conglomerates, including cosmetics, perfumes and accessories, **diffusion ranges** and **licenses**. There is a continuing debate about the viability of haute couture: in 1991 Pierre Bergé, chief executive officer of Yves Saint Laurent, declared that couture would be dead in ten years.

> 'Couture is busy disappearing up its own arse. Modern European high fashion becomes more and more like modern art: inward-looking, elitest and, most damaging of all, laughable.' Colin McDowell (1994)

*Haute couture* seems to be flagging, but in recent years large fashion houses have employed young designers with 'attitude' to revamp their image: for example, John Galliano at Dior, Alexander McQueen at Givenchy, Stella McCartney at Chloé and Michael Kors at Céline. The development of **demi-couture** and *prêt-à-porter* lines, such as Versus (Versace), Miu Miu (Prada) and YSL Rive Gauche, which provide a better return on investment, has also stimulated their fortunes.

The *haute couture* collections are shown in Paris after the *prêt-à-porter* for the same season. Tickets are strictly by invitation only. Because the clothing is made for fewer clients, it does not require the same time-frame and delivery seasons that middle-market or mass manufacturing demands. The clothing is almost always made in-house, at the **atelier**, partly due to the need for fittings and partly for secrecy.

### *Prêt-à-porter* – ready-to-wear

The *prêt-à-porter* collections are organized by the Chambre Syndicale in Paris and shown twice yearly, in January and September. However, unlike the *haute couture* collections, *prêt-à-porter* has competition from ready-to-wear shows in other fashion cities – London, Milan and New York – at approximately the same times. In Paris the standard is very high, and many ranges are diffusion lines of the couture houses or designed by top names. In addition, lower-priced ranges and accessories are shown in an exhibition hall at the Porte de Versailles. Pierre Cardin was the first couturier to show a *prêt-à-porter* collection, in 1959.

Today many designers work both for couture houses and have their own ready-to-wear labels. During the fashion week (now twelve days), some store buyers will see eight or ten shows a day and are bussed from one venue to the next from dawn until midnight. Although in both Paris and London there are official venues for the fashion shows, the designers, especially the up-and-coming ones who show **off-schedule**, often prefer to choose a venue of their own.

### Visiting shows

Understanding the global fashion industry can be challenging, and the best possible insights will come from visiting the fashion cities – both commercial centres and manufacturing areas. It is possible that you will make student trips to London, Paris, Milan or New York for the collections and fabric trade shows (see page 30). Before you go, check fashion websites for up-to-date news on shops and trendy bars and locations. Have some business cards printed to give to any contacts that you may make. Take a sketchbook, camera, phrase book and address book, and a good map for finding off-schedule venues. You will need some smart, fashionable clothes and flat shoes for all the walking you will do.

Colleges are occasionally able to arrange visits to factories and studios as well as to exhibitions, museums and galleries. During the fashion weeks many shops put on additional displays to entice the international fashion pack. Make notes about similarities and differences between the types of merchandise that you find in the stores and boutiques, the **price points** and the displays. Fashion students, especially those following a marketing pathway, will need to be aware of the national styles and trading patterns that affect the marketing of fashion today. Remember that, although the shows and exhibitions may have the glamour and appearance of an entertainment, they are serious professional business events and you should show appropriate respect.

# Time and timing

There is another context, besides geography, that is one of the most powerful forces at work in fashion: time. For the designer of fashion, the key difference between his or her product and that of the designer of almost any other product is shelf life. Fashion has built-in obsolescence. We all require clothing suitable for the different seasons, specific events and even for different times of day. Even though much of the previous formality demanded for work and special events is breaking down, most of us expect to go to weddings in June, take family holidays in August and attend parties in December. Moreover, clothing is often fragile and subject to wear and tear. It needs washing, changing or replacing. Replacement is both a practical and a social requirement. Clothes can only be laundered and patched up so many times; how acceptable our worn clothing is will depend on our age and status. Commerce has capitalized on clothing's obsolescence, and there is an unwritten expectation that we renew our wardrobes, at least partially, in the Spring and Autumn.

In order to supply new clothing when there was a demand, and to make book-keeping and stock records efficient, shops traditionally budgeted for two seasons a year: Spring/Summer and Autumn/Winter. Each of these was followed by a sale period to clear stock quickly and recoup the financial outlay to offset against the next round of payments to suppliers. Designers at the upper end of the market would deliver new collections to the stores and boutiques in January and August. There was often a further delivery of eveningwear for the winter party season in November. The fashion industry has fixed its calendar around this model (see following page).

However, in an increasingly complex world, it can no longer be said that there is truly a 'fashion year'. While most high-fashion businesses observe the traditional calendar, chain stores, which do not sell collections but individual or coordinated items, operate with a tighter turnaround of new items of stock every six to eight weeks from their factories or **private-label** suppliers. In practice, too, the seasons overlap, while some styles, such as winter coats and swimming costumes, are repeated annually. Many companies, for example Armani and Gap, repeat popular styles year after year. In fact, every fashion company will have its own fashion cycle – the calendar by which it plans its ranges, selling, production and delivery set against the demands of the seasons and the waxing and waning of the popularity of designs. This fashion cycle is a complex interlocking of the wheels of the textile and fashion trades (see page 31).

## The show schedule

Fashion is a huge commercial operation, so timing and distribution are crucial to successful sales of a line. The four main centres for fashion design – Paris, London, Milan and New York – all vie with each other for buyers and jostle for time slots on the international fashion-show schedule.

The twice-yearly ready-to-wear fashion-show schedule for buyers has traditionally passed from London to Milan, Paris and then New York over a period of four weeks. For the Spring/Summer collections the schedule usually starts in the second week of September, after the shops have received delivery of the Autumn/Winter lines that were shown the previous March. To complicate matters further, the menswear fashion calendar usually works approximately eight weeks ahead of this plan. Nowadays, however, many designers such as Paul Smith, Yohji Yamamoto and Helmut Lang are producing both menswear and womenswear lines and therefore find it easier to harmonize their shows. Moreover, since the schedule is based on the premise that trends start in Europe, American fashion houses and buyers are increasingly challenging the status quo.

The pressure for time and space on the runway shows during the fashion weeks is immense. Whoever can show first can book their production first and so gain an advantage by delivering early to the stores. To produce two or more collections a year to meet the show deadlines, the fashion designer has to work fast.

# The fashion calendar

| Month | Events | Designer's schedule |
|---|---|---|
| January | Milan – menswear collections for Autumn/Winter<br>Paris – women's collections for Spring/Summer, menswear collections for Autumn/Winter | Finish production of Spring/Summer to deliver to stores end of January. Make sealing samples for Autumn/Winter; negotiate production |
| February | New York – menswear collections for Autumn/Winter<br>Madrid – men's and women's Autumn/Winter collections<br>Florence – Pitti Filati Yarn Show for knitwear<br>Paris – Première Vision Fabric Show<br>Frankfurt – Interstoff Fabric Show | Choose fabrics for Spring/Summer range and begin designing shapes. Preview Autumn/Winter to advance customers – refine collection |
| March | Milan – womenswear designer collections and *moda pronta* exhibition for Autumn/Winter<br>London – womenswear designer collections and ready-to-wear exhibition for Autumn/Winter<br>Paris – womenswear designer collections and *prêt-à-porter* exhibition for Autumn/Winter<br>New York – womenswear market week for Fall 1 delivery | Complete delivery of last Spring/Summer orders and take new Autumn/Winter orders – much liaison with buyers, press and use of research, sales feedback, etc. |
| April | | Make first samples for Spring/Summer range |
| May | Midseason shows – for fast delivery to middle market<br>New York – womenswear market week for Fall 2 delivery | Make samples for Spring/Summer range. Production of Autumn/Winter range |
| June | London – Graduate Fashion Week; catwalk shows of student work; employers take on new staff | Make samples for Spring/Summer range. Production of Autumn/Winter range |
| July | Milan – menswear collections for Spring/Summer<br>Paris – womens couture collections for Autumn/Winter<br>Paris – menswear collections for Spring/Summer<br>Florence – Pitti Filati Yarn Show for knitwear | Make sealing samples for Spring/Summer range. Production of Autumn/Winter range |
| August | New York – menswear collections for Spring/Summer<br>Europe – mills closed for month | Production of Autumn/Winter range. Negotiate production of Spring/Summer range |
| September | Milan – womenswear collections for Spring/Summer<br>Madrid – men's and women's Spring/Summer collections<br>Paris – Première Vision Fabric Show, womenswear collections for Spring/Summer | Deliver Autumn/Winter range to stores. Choose fabrics for following Autumn/Winter – begin designing. Preview Spring/Summer to advance customers – refine range |
| October | London – womenswear collections for Spring/Summer<br>New York – womenswear market for Spring/Summer<br>Midseason shows – for fast delivery to middle market | Complete delivery of Autumn/Winter orders and take new Spring/Summer orders – much liaison with buyers, press and use of research time. Production of Spring/Summer range |
| November | | Deliver holiday and cocktail styles to stores. Design for Autumn/Winter. Production of Spring/Summer range |
| December | Paris – Expofil Exhibition, new colour trends and yarn | Deliver cruise and resort styles to stores. Make samples for Autumn/Winter. Production of Spring/Summer range |

# The fashion cycle

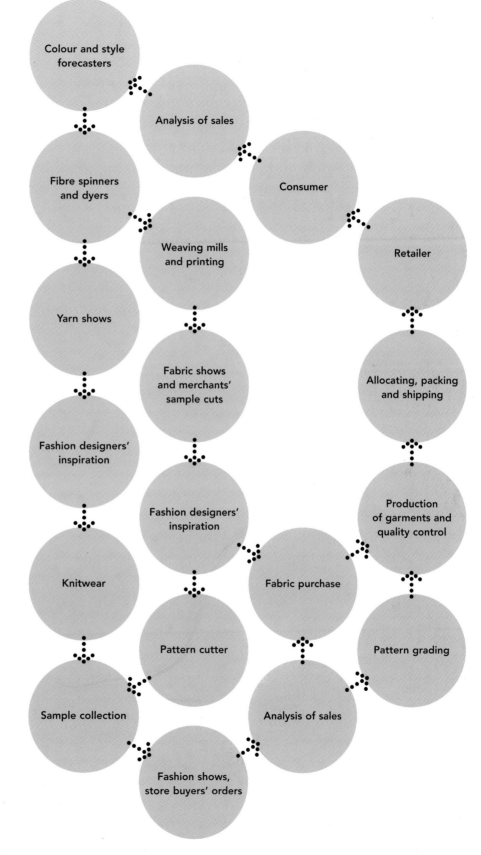

Colour and style forecasters

Analysis of sales

Fibre spinners and dyers

Consumer

Weaving mills and printing

Retailer

Yarn shows

Fabric shows and merchants' sample cuts

Allocating, packing and shipping

Fashion designers' inspiration

Production of garments and quality control

Fashion designers' inspiration

Fabric purchase

Knitwear

Pattern cutter

Pattern grading

Sample collection

Analysis of sales

Fashion shows, store buyers' orders

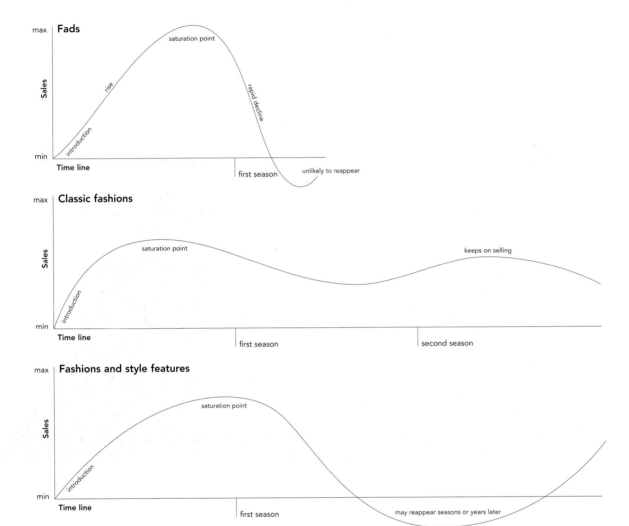

**Fads**

max

Sales

min

saturation point

rise

introduction

rapid decline

Time line

first season

unlikely to reappear

**Classic fashions**

max

Sales

min

saturation point

introduction

keeps on selling

Time line

first season

second season

**Fashions and style features**

max

Sales

min

saturation point

introduction

Time line

first season

may reappear seasons or years later

## Trickle-down effect

Exclusive high culture; movie and pop stars

Those who associate with them, early adopters

Magazine and newspaper readers. Independent shops – first copies

Middle market – goods available in the high street

General public and low culture – goods widely available

## Bubble-up effect

Expensive versions appear in exclusive shops

Fashionistas demand special versions

Magazines, newspapers and TV notice the trend

Middle market gives the trend a name

Street fashion and low culture groups

Designs must be significantly different from those of the previous season in colour and fabrication, yet must maintain some kind of continuity of **handwriting**. New ideas and trends need to be introduced to entice the consumer and excite the press.

In addition, the runway show itself is increasingly becoming an entertainment to which the public has access. London Fashion Week, for example, has extended its schedule in order to feature gala performances of 'highlights' for which the public is able to buy tickets.

'By the time the designers' merchandise has hit their boutiques, the high street will have been there, seen it, done it.' CMT manufacturer Tim Williams

# Fashion and culture

For the designer, knowing what to design and how to present it within the time cycle is not magic or pure intuition, but a matter of good research, planning, experimentation, inspiration and the ability to read cultural trends.

### Tracking trends

Today the fashion professional must be sensitive to developments and events that are taking place globally, in the fashion cities, locally and also in the personal arena. Of the eight motives for wearing clothes outlined at the start of this chapter, psychological self-enhancement and modernity are the two that transform mere clothing into fashion. Most of us wish to continue to look youthful and to fit into the cultural climate of our changing world. Advertising and magazine articles can work on the premise of making us feel inadequate and insecure until we buy into the advocated product or lifestyle. Fashion is a phenomenon that reaches beyond clothing and into the way we choose to spend our leisure time – how we communicate, travel, decorate our homes, eat and generally live our lives.

Observation of what is happening globally – and especially within the micro-world of the target market for which they are designing – is an essential task of designers. Tracking the trends is not necessarily a fully conscious activity but a fine-tuning into the *Zeitgeist* ('spirit of the times'), using a creativity sensibility to shifts of interest in taste. This skill is built up over years and involves the ability to reach back into the memory and make comparisons and construct meanings.

Some clothing items, called **fads**, move very fast through the system, while others (classics) such as the the polo shirt have a slower turnover. Jeans and T-shirts, which have no season, seem to be permanent fixtures, and yet there are subtle variations of fit and stitching, which even the jeans companies can be slow to discern. Sales of Levi's were badly affected when the youth market opted for cargo and combat pants because it wanted a baggier trouser.

### Three cultures

New trends are generally supposed to arise from three main sources: high culture (fine art, literature, classical music, theatre and so on), pop culture (television, pop music, movies and celebrity culture) and low culture (activities pursued locally by special-interest groups outside the mainstream, for example skateboarding). None of these three cultures works in isolation, and each may influence the development of the other.

In his book, *The Theory of the Leisure Class* (1899), the sociologist Thorstein Veblen noted how the 'lower' orders of society emulate their superiors' style of dress as closely as they are able. This cross-cultural emulation is known as the 'trickle-down effect', a phenomenon that merchandisers and designers need to watch carefully if they are to tell what is desirable and what has had its day. Equally of note is the reverse, the 'bubble-up effect', as described by Ted Polhemus in *Streetstyle: From Sidewalk to Catwalk* (1994). In this, styles and activities generated from outside of fashion, by special-interest groups or otherwise marginalized groups, infiltrate the mainstream and come to be seen as new and 'cool'. Mass media such as music and television is largely responsible for the speedy spread of certain popular styles.

Depending on which market or price points you are designing for, these cultural levels will be of variable interest. Trend tracking is not just about looking at clothing within these sources but about changes in demographics, behaviour and the way people live their lives. This consumer analysis can give us a picture of the kind of clothing and accessories that people will need to accompany them in the future (see Chapter II).

### Fashion forecasting

The designer not only has all the same opportunities that the public has to absorb the current trends, mores and cultural pursuits, but he or she is also supported by fashion forecasting – a small but lucrative scion of the fashion industry itself. Fashion forecasters are market-research specialists and analysts who offer financial services and illustrated reports to the fashion manufacturers for a fee. Predictions are built up through exhaustive statistical surveys to gauge the relative popularity of fabrics, colours, details and features. Some companies employ trend-chasers or 'cool-hunters', individuals who are especially good at discerning trends in their early stages and predicting products that will fit into that image. Many forecasting companies also put together style books and specifications of the prevailing and emerging styles, with predictions and suggestions for the next season. The largest trend-forecasting companies employ more fashion designers than most clothing companies do.

# Media

Fashion journalists and the celebrity-mad news media – including magazines, television and the internet – now all report on the major fashion events and designer shows. At one time these were comparatively private, invitation-only affairs. Information leaked out through the filter of the few invited upmarket journalists, and sometimes reached the outside world months later. Nowadays fashion shows are media circuses, principally staged to generate interest and catch the interest of the media.

### The press

The editors of newspapers and fashion magazines such as Anna Wintour, Franca Sozzani and Doris Wiedemann at US, Italian and German *Vogue* and Suzy Menkes at the *International Herald Tribune* have tremendous power and are courted enthusiastically by designers and model agencies. The editors advise us how to wear the

# Fashion time line

| Date and key events | Designers of influence | Silhouette and style |
| --- | --- | --- |
| **Late 18th century**<br>1775–90 American Declaration of Independence; French Revolution | Rose Bertin, dressmaker to Marie Antoinette; tailor Andre Scheling. Sumptuary laws and wealth dictated appropriate dress until the rise of the bourgeoisie | Luxurious brocades, wide-hipped panniers, corsets and wigs gave way to shepherdess styles and plain unadorned fabrics in patriotic colours for men and women |
| **19th century**<br>1780–1815 Napoleonic Empire; Battle of Waterloo; Industrial Revolution | Hippolyte Leroy; tailor to the Empress Josephine. Romantic eclecticism of the court of King George IV, influenced by Beau Brummel | High waisted chemises, narrow Empire line dresses. Indian cashmeres and American cottons. Bonnets and millinery. Regency high collars, breeches, frock-coats, frills and flamboyance |
| 1830–1865 Invention of photography and sewing and knitting machines. Britain is the centre of industry and world trade; France is the centre of art and culture | Charles Frederick Worth dressed Empress Eugénie and Queen Victoria. | Puff sleeves, low necklines, bell shapes, the crinoline and corsetry at its most extreme during the reign of Queen Victoria (1837–1901). Less flamboyant menswear; white shirts, waistcoats, frockcoats, trousers, boots |
| Late 1800s Invention of lightbulb, telephone and radio; 1889 *Vogue* magazine launched; department stores open in cities | Redfern, Paquin, Doucet, Lucile. Creed and Henry Poole tailored menswear | Broad breast and bustles, draped skirts, bloomers for sports. Working women wear practical 'Gibson Girl' separates. Introduction of the brassiere. Men wear suits with a long trouser |
| **20th century**<br>Russian Revolution; Women's Suffrage; Public transport and air travel | Jeanne Lanvin, Callot Soeurs, Fortuny Paul Poiret. Rise of female designers, training schemes for dressmakers | Disappearance of corsets; S-shaped silhouette gives way to chemise. Hobble skirts followed by looser styles due to motor car and mobility. Lampshade tunics, drapery. No waist. Use of new fibre – rayon |
| 1914–18 World War I; cinema popularized | Delaunay, Bakst, Lelong. Influence of modern art, Fauves, Cubists, Vorticists | Emancipation and revolutionary styles, square cuts. Increasing sobriety in menswear. Suits and practical dress |
| 1920s Weimar Republic in Germany; prohibition in the USA; invention of television and gramophone | Vionnet, Gres, Ricci, Patou | Boyish look: flat-chested, low waists, bias cuts, women wear short hair. Jazz and nightclub life; short skirts for dancing. Baggy men's suits |
| 1926 General Strike in Britain<br>1929 Black Friday stockmarket crash | Chanel | Trade depression, longer bodylines, figure-skimming silhouette, 'tea dresses'. New fibres. Influence of Hollywood stars |
| 1930s<br>1936–9 Spanish Civil War<br>1937 King Edward VIII abdicates | Mainbocher, Schiaparelli, Adrian, Balenciaga, Molyneux, Hartnell | Precision grooming. Detailed suits. Extremes of wealth and poverty. Princess line, belted and waisted, sensible shoes, suits |
| 1940s<br>1939–45 World War II; atomic bomb | Creed, Hardy Amies, the rise of American designers: Blass, Cashin, McCardle, James, Norell | Practical, quasi-military, womens' trousers, 'make do and mend' approach, platform shoes |
| 1947 Synthetic dyes introduced | Dior's 'New Look', Couture houses Chanel, Givenchy, Balmain and Fath reopen. Italian industry revives | Sophistication, concave posture. Hourglass silhouette, fuller, longer skirts, nylon stockings, accessorized ensembles. Lightweight, easy-care synthetic fabrics |
| 1950s<br>Queen Elizabeth II; availability of domestic washing machines | Belville Sassoon, Hardy Amies. Italian designers: Pucci, Ferragamo, Cerruti | New 'youth market', girlish looks (Audrey Hepburn and Juliette Greco), full skirts, sweaters, flat shoes. Unisex styles. Rock and roll, denim and gingham |

| | | |
|---|---|---|
| **1960s**<br>Cuban Revolution<br>1963 President Kennedy assassinated; transatlantic telephone cable | Saint Laurent, Cardin, Courrèges, Rabanne. First generation of art-school trained designers: Thea Porter, Jean Muir, Foale and Tuffin | The sack shape, knee length skirts, Chanel suits, Rebels, Beatniks and the Beatles. The sharply-tailored Italian suit for men and trouser suits for women |
| 1965 Vietnam War; Space Race; Cold War | London designers and boutiques: Mary Quant, Biba, Bus Stop, Mr Freedom | Mini skirts, PVC and paper dresses, colourful geometric prints, tights, influence of Pop Art on fashion. Cult of the fashion photographer and 'dolly bird' models: Twiggy and Shrimpton |
| 1967 The Summer of Love<br>1968 Paris riots<br>1969 Moon landing | Influence of Paris couture wanes. Bill Gibb, Ossie Clarke, Zandra Rhodes | Hippie movement, Eastern styles: 'maxi' skirts, long hair, florals, embroidery, beads, suede, cheesecloth. Colour and flamboyance returns to menswear |
| **1970s**<br>1974 Nixon and Watergate scandal | Halston, Gucci, Fiorucci, Anthony Price versus Katharine Hamnett, Perry Ellis, Ralph Lauren | Glamour versus Feminism – disco fashion, sexy and glittery versus flat chests, Doc Martens flat shoes, dungarees, jeans. Power dressing, Chanel suits and shoulder pads, big hair |
| 1979 Margaret Thatcher becomes first female Prime Minister | Vivienne Westwood, Body Map, John Galliano | Fashion makes an alliance with youth music. Punk, anti-fashion, bondage and fetish clothing, street fashions |
| **1980s**<br>1982 Falklands War; video and MTV | High fashion becomes increasingly international: Adolfo Dominguez, Calvin Klein, Donna Karan, Armani, Missoni, Versace, Alaia, Lagerfeld, Lacroix, Gaultier, Gigli, Valentino, Jil Sander, Kenzo | Street versus high style epitomized by icons Madonna and Princess Diana. Cult of the healthy body, sportswear, stretch jersey. Travel and work favours 'easy dressing'. |
| 1985 Live Aid<br>Late 1980s AIDS; Tiananmen Square massacre | Japanese designers: Issey Miyake, Yohji Yamamoto, Rei Kawakubo. Belgian designers: Dries Van Noten, Ann Demeulemeester | Counter-cultural, anti-excess clothing expressing intellectual and artistic aesthetic. Loose, architectural cuts, black, worn with flat shoes |
| 1989 Fall of the Berlin Wall | Rise of international high street labels: Esprit, Benetton, Gap, H&M | Supermodels and celebrities popularize casual sportswear and jeans. Trainers. Natural silhouette |
| **1990s**<br>1991 Gulf War; Apartheid ends<br>1993 Personal computers widely available | Growth of designer labels owned by fashion conglomerates. Brand awareness. rebirth of labels: Prada, Hermès, Gucci, Fendi. Great diversity of styles widely available | Trade recession, grunge and deconstructed styles, ecologically friendly fibres, recycling, anti-fur. Oversized silhouettes, androgyny. Revivals of 1960s' and 1970s' fashions. Glamour versus conceptual fashion |
| 1997 China reclaims Hong Kong; death of Princess Diana | Postmodern designers: Martin Margiela, Helmut Lang, Hussein Chalayan | East opens gates for international manufacturing. Trade barriers dissolve. Internet speeds communication. High-tech production. Return of the bias dress and high heels, feminine styles |
| **21st century**<br>2001 Destruction of World Trade Center in New York by terrorists | British and American designers working in Paris couture: John Galliano, Alexander McQueen, Julien Macdonald, Stella McCartney, Tom Ford and Michael Kors | Eclecticism, individualism, fashion as a spectacle. Dismantling of the glamorous myth. Backlash against mass-market labels, Revival of craft techniques |

**From acceptance to obsolescence**

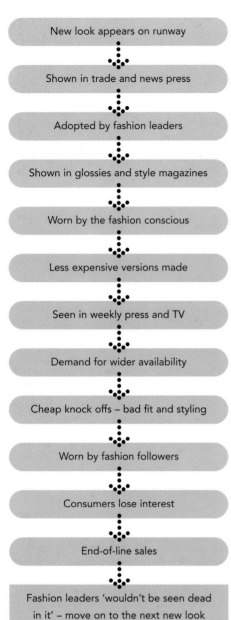

New look appears on runway

Shown in trade and news press

Adopted by fashion leaders

Shown in glossies and style magazines

Worn by the fashion conscious

Less expensive versions made

Seen in weekly press and TV

Demand for wider availability

Cheap knock offs – bad fit and styling

Worn by fashion followers

Consumers lose interest

End-of-line sales

Fashion leaders 'wouldn't be seen dead in it' – move on to the next new look

new styles and frequently show examples of mainstream equivalents. Accessories, beauty, hair and make-up are all adjusted to complete the season's look.

The public usually becomes aware of the new trends and styles in fashion immediately before the chief selling seasons. The spring (February/March) and autumn (August/September) issues of the monthly magazines carry large editorials and often produce supplements showing the international collections that were shown three months earlier at the Paris, Milan, London and New York shows.

Fashion designers regularly buy the magazines that target the market sectors they are interested in. If their public relations (PR) agent has been successful in placing their garments in features, they will have press cards made and sent out to their stockists to encourage further sales. They will also look for listings of the stockists of their competitors' product so that they can make overtures to them the following season.

## Trade publications

More important than the 'glossies' for the designer are the trade magazines; although it is important to check who and what is being covered, much of what appears in the general press is already out of date. Trade magazines cover all industry events and fashion shows. In the United States, the daily newspaper for the fashion industry, *Women's Wear Daily*, reports in depth on a particular segment of the market each weekday. Besides giving general news, it also has statistical breakdowns and lists of suppliers and manufacturers, as well as a classified jobs section.

In the United Kingdom, *Drapers Record* fulfils a similar task. Quarterly magazines such as *International Textiles* feature upcoming fabric stories. *Textile View*, *Viewpoint* and *View Colour* are beautifully produced colour magazines that are full of reports, fashion forecasting and fabric developments. Some or all of these publications may be held in libraries.

## The internet

For the fashion student, using the internet is a highly time- and cost-effective way of finding fabrics, trimmings and manufacturing expertise. Having found a likely supplier on the internet, it is usually also possible to email the company and place an order. There are a growing number of fashion industry resources that are not accessible to the public but which are available through colleges that license their limited use by students. The following internet resources are also useful: live and archived news; virtual collections of costume museums around the world; fashion e-zines; fashion-oriented bulletin boards and chatrooms (good for contacts and job hunting); e-commerce and e-tail sites; promotional sites, which may include information on a company's history, showcase past or current collections, or web-stream its fashion shows.

# From manufacture to market II

# Historical background

The mass production of clothing was made possible by the invention of the sewing machine in 1829. Menswear and military uniforms were among the first pieces of clothing to be produced on sewing machines. In 1850 Levi Strauss started making denim workman's trousers for American prospectors. Material was cut and made up into individual bundles and sent out to the homes of machinists to be made up. Later, to save time and costs of delivery and collection, and to ensure the continuity of quality, machinists who were willing to work outside the home were brought together in factories.

However, it was with the introduction of the foot-treadle machine in 1859 by the American inventor Isaac Singer, that the sewing machine began to play a serious role both in the home and the workplace. The Industrial Revolution in Britain and Europe had developed working practices for speed and efficiency, especially in fabric production and ceramics. Both industries employed large female workforces. Factory-floor managers soon found that if a worker was shown how to do just one or two parts of the garment then it could be made very speedily, as the piece was passed down the line for the next stage of the process. This became known as 'piece work' or 'section work', and is still the most common system of production today.

Electric sewing machines appeared on the market in 1921. This greatly increased the output of women's clothing and enabled mainstream shops to stock the same lines all over the country. Uniformity and perfection of finish was such a novelty that it rendered the term 'home-made' derogatory for the first time. In the United States, the largest proportion of mass-produced clothing was sold through catalogues and mail order.

During World War II, trade was disrupted in Europe and all possible manufacturing facilities were turned over to war-related production. The larger factories were subsidized and organized by the government for streamlined productivity. After the war this left them in a stronger position to continue to produce in high volume. Many smaller factories floundered or died. The United Kingdom has been left a legacy of factories built to handle high-volume, medium-quality clothing rather than small runs. Conversely, in Italy and France, which were more heavily damaged by war, grants from the United States and the Common Market encouraged the growth of family businesses and other small units, which flourished into a network of high-quality producers.

# Manufacture today

In recent years the most dramatic changes in manufacturing have been in pattern-cutting, grading and tracking distribution and sales through computer-operated systems. For example, at the lower end of the market, new technology allows the cutting, fusing and stitching of a standard-sized suit in approximately ninety minutes. (By contrast, a bespoke suit, with up to 200 hand-finishing operations, may take up to three days to complete.) Suits can also be made to individual measurements and laser-cut, using computer-aided design (CAD) technology. Some CAD machinery will create hydraulic 'cookie-cutter' dies for garments, such as jeans, which will be made in thousands. Similarly, recent innovations in computer-aided 'integral knitting'

**Top and above** The industrial sample machinist has a very broad knowledge of garment-making techniques, unlike the piece worker who makes the same item many times over.

**Opposite** The lock-stitch sewing machine quickly became the mainstay of the production line in the fashion industry.

# THE BEST MACHINES
## FOR
## TAILORS.

Machines for all purposes connected with Tailoring.

**LABOUR SAVING.**    **INCREASED OUTPUT.**    **ECONOMICAL PRODUCTION.**

The TABLE shown is a very convenient and popular form for the use of Tailors and Manufacturers handling large quantities of material in irregular form.

With End and Back Leaves down the Table is 38 inches long by 19 inches wide. With both leaves up it is 48 inches long by 25 inches wide, thus affording ample room for easy and convenient handling of large quantities of work.

**SINGER MACHINE 31K.**

THE BOBBIN HAS A CAPACITY FOR 100 YARDS OF No. 60 COTTON.

High Speed. Lock Stitch. Specially Designed for Durability, Stitch Perfection and General Utility.

FOR CASH, OR EASY TERMS OF PAYMENT CAN BE ARRANGED.

# Singer Sewing Machine Co. Ltd.
SHOPS IN EVERY CITY.

The high rates of wages can only be counterbalanced by using labour-saving devices to secure increased production.

**Above** Knitting has evolved from the use of two needles to complex computer-driven machinery. A knitwear designer will learn to use both.

**Right** Ribbons are stored within easy reach.

by Japanese engineers have led to the manufacture of entire knitted garments, complete with collars and pockets, within forty-five minutes. Stretch fibre and fabric development has also led to the shape-moulding and engineering of underwear that is lightweight yet strong, giving different types of localized support but requiring much less stitching and skill to assemble. The fully automated assembly line for fashion exists, particularly in hosiery and sports-clothing factories. On the whole, however, it is difficult for robots to handle flexible fabrics and they make mistakes when unsupervised.

The speeding-up of many small processes has allowed the industry to respond rapidly to market demands; this is known as Just In Time (**JIT**) manufacturing. In the 1990s many of the larger American suppliers worked with the store groups to set up computerized electronic point-of-sale (**EPOS**) technology. Using the universal product code (**UPC**) – a bar-coding system that identifies style, size and colour – they were able to track their sales and replace or move goods around speedily and much more efficiently. Better data also results in better financial planning for the following round of purchasing.

A consequence of this is that stores are now less willing to tie up their funds in large stocks, and prefer manufacturers who offer them goods quickly or on less risky 'sale-or-return' and concession terms. The period between order and delivery to the stores is approximately ten weeks in the middle market. This period can be cut considerably, provided that there is fabric in stock and if the factory delivers in drops or sized packages rather than waiting for the whole order to be made up.

**Top left** A machine reads the pattern shape and size so that it can be made into a laser-cutting marker.

**Centre left** Trimmings such as zips, tapes and buttons are bought in large quantities.

**Bottom left** A stock of regular fabrics can be quickly made into popular styles. Fabric is mounted onto spreading machines so that many layers can be cut at once.

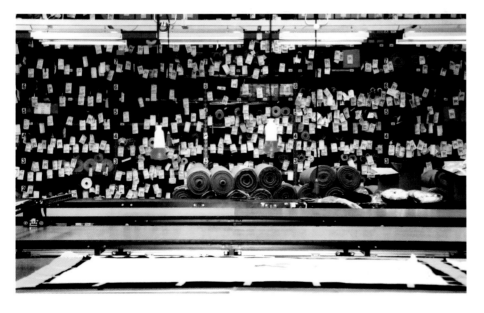

# Types of producer

Whatever the market sector or category of clothing, it is essential that the designer and pattern-cutter work together within the framework of the capabilities of the manufacturing available to them. They must be aware of the best that manufacturers or producers can do within the limits of their technological and human resources. There is nothing more frustrating for a designer than discovering too late that a good design cannot be reproduced at the quality or price required.

> 'What's so good about perfection anyway? I don't like it myself. I want to see something a little bit different. I don't want my things to be the same as anyone else's…' Designer Shelley Fox

The fashion industry consists of three main types of producers: manufacturers, wholesalers and contractors.

### Manufacturers

Sometimes known as vertical producers, manufacturers handle all operations such as buying the fabric, designing or buying in designs, making the garments and selling and delivering the finished garments. The advantage of this method is good quality control and brand exclusivity, but it often creates high overheads. Vertical companies usually specialize in offering fabric, fashion and classic clothing to the larger stores and chains. Some may even have their own retail outlets, but most deal only in wholesale goods.

Manufacturers can grow to a fair size, but many are smaller businesses that rely on the talents of craft-oriented designers. These include *haute couture* and bespoke tailoring firms, which make their products in-house. In this instance garments are 'one-offs' and may require numerous fittings, so it is appropriate that the designer and cutter work in close proximity with the machinists. Production is limited to what can be managed by a small but skilled workforce and priced accordingly. Pleating, embroidery, buttonholing and finishes that require specialist machinery are usually subcontracted. Couturiers and bespoke tailors often operate from a single premises, with a shop at the front and workrooms at the back.

**Right** A pattern-cutter tests the bias lay of a pattern. There is much more waste fabric than if the pieces were to be laid parallel to the selvedge.

**Opposite** A sample is cut and made in the factory to send to the manufacturer for approval.

## Wholesalers (or 'jobbers')

Many top fashion-design companies come into this category because, while they produce the designs, buy materials and plan the cutting, selling and delivery, they do not actually make the clothing. This system gives wholesalers the flexibility to make innovative clothing in small runs by subcontracting CMT units (see page 46). However, smaller companies run the risk of being put to the bottom of the priority list by contractors working with larger orders. They also have less control over quality, price and **knock offs**. On the other hand, **jobbers** do not have the high wage bills or machinery problems typical of manufacturers. In order to justify the higher prices of their clothing, they need to spend more on advertising, trade and fashion shows, and stylish premises.

### The docket

Before a designer or client places an order with a contractor he or she will want to see how well the design-room sample can be reproduced. The contractor will cut and make one or more samples for approval. Once refinements, details and cost have been agreed, the chosen sample is 'sealed' as the agreed reference garment, together with a specification sheet. In the past, the **sealing sample** had a metal seal affixed to it in order to prevent switches being made in the event of a dispute.

When manufacturers or contractors receive a confirmed order from a designer or store, it is called a **docket**, a form showing a breakdown of the numbers of garments required in different sizes. Traditionally this has been rounded up to 'dozens', twelve dozen making a gross – often the minimum for an order. Clothes are usually labelled, given swing-tickets and inspected before the finished order, also known as a docket, leaves the factory in vans equipped with hanging rails. At the wholesaler's warehouse they will be allocated against the shop orders and **kimballed**: that is, tagged with information or price tags before being dispatched to the shops.

**Above** Patterns are often coded using different coloured card for size or collection.

**Above centre** Garments are pressed before being prepared for dispatch.

**Above right** Garments ready for dispatch. Different styles and sizes will be 'pulled' to fill an order.

**Below** The pattern lay-plan, or marker, is a template for the cutter to follow. In order to keep the profit margin of a garment it must use the least amount of fabric.

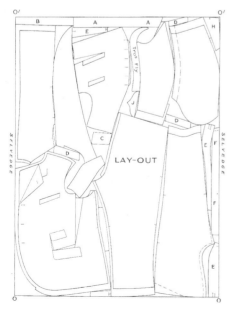

## Contractors

Contractors vary in size from well-established large-scale operators – often referred to as 'the big boys' – through medium Cut, Make and Trim (CMT) workshops to the lone **outworker**. Large contract manufacturers are located mostly in or near industrial towns, which is helpful for the distribution of goods. They have design teams which work to an agreed framework negotiated by the store outlets that they supply. They are responsible for all aspects of production, from pattern-making, production and trimming to packaging and delivery.

Contractors do not produce collections but small groups and **stories** designed around a silhouette, fabric or perceived market demand. The design teams produce a great many samples. Some are market tested in flagship stores, and those that show promise are chosen by store selectors or merchandisers. These are finished with the stores' own label and are not offered to other customers. In the United States this is called a **private label**. Contractors take on the risks of design and manufacturing, but not those of failed sales. They negotiate complex rolling contracts with the chains they supply, worked out well in advance of the season, as a lack of orders could put them out of business.

Cut, Make and Trim (CMT) factories tend to be small, family-run businesses employing fewer than thirty people. They are often subcontracted by the larger manufacturers at busy times, but they also work for independent design companies. These factories vary enormously in their expertise and reliability. Some have areas of specialism, such as lingerie or special machinery. CMT units do not supply patterns, cloth or trimmings, although they will press, hang, bag or box goods. They do not take on the design or sales risks and may use outworkers when busy.

Outworkers are usually women working from home. They are often very skilled, and set aside a part of the home as a workspace. Outworkers are used by independent designers who have work dockets too small for CMT units. A designer will usually supply them with a set of cut bundles, thread and trimmings and negotiate and pay for the sewing. If the same style is placed with more than one outworker, consistency of style or delivery can be problematic.

**Offshore production**

Today many jobbers use offshore production. Manufacturing in the United Kingdom, Europe and the United States is expensive in comparison to production in the Far East and in other regions with low wages or heavily subsidized industries. The quality control, speed of production and care taken over the finishing and trimming can be extremely high. In the 1990s the American designer Calvin Klein moved all of his production to the Far East and was quickly followed by other fashion houses. Large companies employ agencies and brokers to negotiate and oversee production and ensure that schedules and standards are met.

There is widespread ethical disapproval of out-sourcing labour. Many consumers are uncomfortable with the knowledge that well-known labels have clothing made by cheap and exploitative labour based in 'sweatshops', although most people still prefer to pay less for their clothing. Some manufacturers have been the target of boycotts, demonstrations and protests for their employment policies. This in turn has led to trade quotas, tariff embargoes and 'banana wars' against goods such as cashmere sweaters.

Hong Kong – then a British colony – was the first country to which Europeans and Americans turned for ready-to-wear production. Backed by a social ethos that favoured efficiency and cost-effectiveness, a willing labour market and continuously upgraded technology, Hong Kong quickly became the second-largest exporter of clothing after Italy. Today there are approximately 10,000 factories of varying sizes in Hong Kong.

With so many companies trading globally today, cost is no longer the priority; the crucial issue is timing. There is such a demand for new fashion that it must be brought to the market fast or perish. The manufacturers in China, Taiwan and Korea can respond with speed, quality and technological organization. American fashion companies look for a turnaround time from Hong Kong agents of about 1,000 hours – from the recognition of a new style to the delivery of some 10,000 garments – and all from 10,000 miles away.

'We do four seasons – spring, summer, fall and holiday – and two lines in the spring and fall. There are 170 pieces per line of which 30 per cent is knitwear made in the Far East. The line gets edited down and about 100 styles get dropped. It's like doing a degree show four times a year. The pressure is intense but with the right people it's fun. The key to it is organization…' Knitwear designer for Ralph Lauren

# Market segmentation

The fashion and clothing industry is segmented broadly into three distinct divisions: womenswear, menswear and childrenswear. Womenswear is the largest segment, taking close to 57 per cent of the market share, followed by a fast-growing 24 per cent share in menswear. Childrenswear is the smallest segment.

In order to develop a sales strategy and promotional plans, manufacturers and wholesalers have to analyse the market in depth, breaking the three main segments into smaller ones. Analysts identify market segments not only by age, gender and socioeconomic groupings but also by attitudes.

## Identifying target markets

Market analysts consider the following significant factors in identifying target markets:

*Age* This grouping helps retailers to determine people's buying habits by the life stage they are likely to be going through. Knowing the population numbers within each age group helps to calculate the potential size of the market. In the UK and the US, the fashion conscious 15–24 age range is declining in number, while the 25–34 age range represents the largest market.

*Gender* Until recently most menswear and womenswear shops were separate. Now that more men are shopping, there is a trend to include both in the large chains and casualwear stores.

*Demographics* The study of population distribution can track socioeconomic groupings, ethnicity, income levels and use of leisure time across a country. Different clothing will be required in a sleepy country town than in a lively holiday resort. Ethnic groups may have preferences for certain colours, brands and accessories.

*Lifestyle* How people live and travel affects the clothing they require. For example, career women require separates, business clothes and classics. Single men take more interest in sports.

*Physical characteristics* Size is related to genetic factors that may be dominant in various locations. Surveys show that the Western population is in general getting taller and heavier.

*Psychographics* Psychographics is the study of fashion attitudes, whether people are fashion-active and early or late adopters of styles. City dwellers will tend to pick up on new styles faster than those living in rural areas.

*Social class* People like to be seen to belong to a particular level of society and to shop with their peers. For example, Harvey Nichols department store in London is considered the epitome of upper-middle-class chic. In New York, analysts have designated people as either 'uptown' or 'downtown' shoppers.

*Social behaviour* Broad changes in society, such as a higher rate of divorce and the creation of single-parent families, can affect people's spending power.

*Values and attitudes* These are subtle lifestyle indicators that help marketers determine how to fine-tune sales and advertising material. Surveys are done to collate people's responses to many subjects such as dating and sex, movies and music, current affairs and politics.

*Economic circumstances* Salary is not the same as disposable income – a high-earning middle-class family may spend its money on private education for the children rather than on clothing. The availability of credit or the cost of mortgage repayments will also affect clothing purchases.

*Religion* Religious observance may influence the buying of modest or flamboyant clothing among certain communities, or create more demand for expensive wedding outfits. It may mean that in some neighbourhoods the shops do not open on particular days of the week or during festivals.

'Only those retailers who are positioned to serve a carefully targeted market niche with a distinctive and differentiated offering will prosper.'
MTI/EMAP report (1999)

Retail managers will deduce the profile of their actual customers or target customers by counting and observing who comes through the door. In the 1980s the use of the newly developed electronic point-of-sale (EPOS) technology enabled the tracking and replacement of items that were selling well. Slow-moving goods were quickly withdrawn so that shops were stocked with desirable merchandise. Sizes that were running out could be restocked quickly. This feedback is known as matrix marketing.

Statistics compiled from national census data, economic conditions, market analysis and shop retail performance can be charted to show broad trends. This kind of work has shown, for example, that sales of suits and outerwear have generally given way to sports clothing for both men and women; the jeans market is in decline; the independent shop is losing out to the concessions, in-store designer ranges and high-fashion diffusion lines; there is a growing awareness of branding and brand loyalty; teenagers are much more demanding of street-fashion styles and shoes; women's sizes are getting larger.

In the past the majority of manufacturers and the shops they supplied focused on a particular sort of product such as day dresses, men's shirts or eveningwear. A similar categorization was used in department stores, with, for example, all knitwear grouped together. Now, store merchandisers group garments either by the age, lifestyle and socioeconomic group formula, or by fashion houses, which often offer an entire colour- and fabric-coordinated 'story'.

Independent shops can offer a unique ambience tailored to local customers, as well as providing personal attention.

# Types of retailer

### Shop reports

As a student of fashion you will learn to do shop reports. This is essentially a technique that will train your interest in market sectors, sales environments, consumers and trend-spotting. It demands a practised, evaluative eye for noting the evolution of trends and manufacturing finishes, colours and styles that are shifting or being marked down, price points and introductions of new fabrics, sizes and labels. The purpose of this kind of market intelligence is not to copy, as the designs are already out there, but to check the time frame for styles, avoid the pitfalls of overexposing a design, check manufacturing benchmarks and gain inspiration for developing the positive trends. Use a notebook, and ask questions of sales staff and customers discreetly.

Today, shopping can be said to be the primary leisure activity. The demand for certain types of clothing and the most convenient or pleasing ways of shopping for them will be reflected by the success or failure of forms of retail. The fashion student needs to be aware of what the different retail environments aim to provide and what the constraints of each are.

### Independents

Retailers with fewer than ten outlets make up this category. Most are sole traders with only one shop or boutique. In the United States these are known as 'mom-and-pop stores' because they can offer the personal touch and often specialize

**Right** The smaller store is often willing to take the risk of stocking new designers' collections because they need to differentiate their merchandise from the chain stores.

**Opposite** Concessions help to fill a department store with variety. The department store reassures the shopper with its wide range of goods and reputation for reliability and service.

in certain categories of clothing. Independent shops are more pressured by the high cost of business rates and rents than the larger chains. Independent shops are usually not in prime sites because of the cost. There are fewer independent menswear stores, although this is a growing area and is fast catching up with a declining women's independent sector. Independents have to stock different goods than the bigger stores; they have higher costs so they need strong fashion innovation, designer names or exclusivity to draw in customers. Independents have less control over suppliers than department stores with larger budgets and greater influence to determine when, and at what price, they will buy or mark down stock.

## Multiples

These are chains of shops, or several chains owned by a parent company, and they include well-known names such as French Connection and Gap. Some specialize in one particular area, while others provide a wide variety of merchandise. They own or lease prime city centre or shopping-mall sites and therefore generate a high turnover. They are able to buy in bulk or commission own-label merchandise and distribute it to branches. Multiples build brand familiarity and loyalty with corporate image and logo, packaging and advertising. The customer expects to find moderate fashion with middle price points. They add value with customer lures such as cafés, store cards and promotions.

## Department stores

Department stores offer a wide variety of goods on different floors, or departments, and are designed to keep the customer in the store for as long as possible. When they first appeared in the late nineteenth century, department stores were distinguished by their magnificent architecture and interiors, and their prime locations. Typically, some 70 per cent of the merchandise on sale is fashion. Many stores offer loyalty cards that provide retailers with information for their customer databases and allow them to target specific groups with promotional information. Department stores feature **concession** trading and a wide choice of goods. They also offer extra facilities, such as toilets, restaurants, credit cards, banking facilities and wedding-gift services. Today, department stores are having to work very hard to redress an old-fashioned image and ambience that is unpopular with young shoppers.

The shopping mall offers accessibility and protection from the elements. Many have dynamic architectural and leisure features which encourage people to visit and stay all day.

## Concessions

Department stores used to buy in all their goods from manufacturers and jobbers. The main advantages of buying in goods are diversity of product and no manufacturing costs. Tying up money in stock is expensive and risky; a store must make a profit within a seasonal time frame or it will be unable to purchase the fashions that its customers expect for the following period. If the buyers make mistakes in forecasting, or if the weather and other variable conditions change consumer interest, unsold stock has to be heavily discounted in the sales.

Concessions take the risk out of retail. The store lets out space to a retailer or manufacturer for a fixed percentage of turnover. The agreement guarantees the store a minimum percentage of income. The concessionaire employs his or her own sales staff, provides fixtures and fittings and is responsible for stock and changing displays. Concessions work particularly well for the small pitches of accessory and cosmetic companies. Opening a concession in a busy store is a popular way for young designers to get a foothold on the retail ladder and test the market for various styles without the risks and high costs of opening a shop.

## Franchises

Franchising is a low-risk method of retailing. Essentially, franchise companies are well-established firms which make the stock, distribute the goods, provide advertising, display material and a company **fascia** or logo. The **franchisee** buys the right to sell those goods within a specified geographical area for an initial fee and further royalty payments. The prices are set at the same levels for all the franchises. In return for a smaller proportion of the profits, the parent manufacturing company gets wide distribution of products and a consistent market presence without having to manage local sales and staffing issues.

## Discounters

Discounters buy stock at reduced rates from a wide variety of international sources, especially where manufacturing costs are low or contractors wish to dispose of **cabbage** (excess fabric), cancelled orders and overproduction. They have grown to take a 15 per cent share of the market because they offer very competitive prices. It is customary for the discounter to remove the labels so that shoppers are unable to identify the makers of the clothing.

## Factory shops

Factory shops developed from the overstocks and faulty goods produced by a manufacturer that were offered at reduced prices to employees. Eventually manufacturers opened to the public. The recession of the 1980s saw a steep proliferation of factory outlets, and in some areas they have left the factory premises and grouped together with others to create smart out-of-town shopping 'villages', offering both high quality and low cost. Customers tend to be in the top socio-economic groups, with large cars and high budgets.

## Markets

The vibrant and informal environment of the market is where people traditionally expect to find a bargain. The fashion goods sold on market stalls tend to be from similar sources as those of the discounters. Damaged or rejected goods known as seconds are offered cheaply to market traders. Goods are customarily exchanged for cash, and the usual consumer protections concerning 'merchantable quality'

**Left and above** Many designers gain experience of customer demand by making and selling their own accessories or clothes on market stalls.

are not strictly observed. Some alternative markets attract young designers and students wishing to capitalize on their talents and test out their target audience. Flea markets such as London's Portobello Road and the Porte de Clignancourt in Paris, which specialize in second-hand goods, can be rich sources of inspiration and of beautiful antique fabrics for students.

## Mail order

Mail-order shopping suits those who cannot, or do not wish to, go shopping. It has been popular since the early American settlers needed goods to run their remote ranches, and Sears and Roebuck filled the demand for workwear and home furnishings. Catalogues were mailed out twice a year and shoppers were offered attractive payment by instalment terms. Mail order is an expanding field; many working women no longer have the time to shop. Many retail conglomerates also run mail-order businesses. 'Magalogues' – catalogues in the form of monthly magazines – are the latest marketing tool of suppliers and department stores.

## Electronic shopping

Electronic shopping is a development of mail order made possible by recent technology. People can shop over the internet through their computer or even through their televisions using digital technology. Retailing on the internet is proving to be lucrative for some sectors such as books, music and hobbyist items. Womenswear is under-represented, although simple items such as T-shirts, casual sportswear and hi-tech clothing do well. One of the advantages of internet shopping is that shopping is international and open twenty-four hours to credit-card customers.

# Price points

Price points for fashion merchandise are related to the quality of manufacture, availability, design content and the demographic target group. The balance between these diverse factors is not always easy to discern and may turn up some apparent oddities. For example, street-style fashion may be cutting-edge, not widely available and reasonably well-made, yet, seemingly against logic, it sells at a comparatively low cost; this is because the people who are interested in it are few in number and do not belong to a high-income group.

> 'Costing is important, you have to run your business properly and make a profit. But you also have to take risks, calculated risks … Our best-selling fabric last winter was £52.00 a metre (about $72 a yard); that is very expensive by the time it is marked up.' Designer Joe Casely-Hayford

As a designer you must be aware of the prices set by your nearest competitors. Prices must be fair and reflect the value of the fabric and manufacturing style you have employed. You should also be aware of any extra incentives that are offered to the buyer in the way of credit facilities, sale-or-return privileges, special promotional goods and advertising support. The retail buyers will be making comparisons as they order each season and will also be aware of price resistance in the shop. Retailers must pitch their price bands just right for their customers, even at sale time. Steep mark-ups force the customer to shop around for better value, while dramatic discounts make the customer very sceptical of the original price. Establishing an upper and lower level that is acceptable is as important as the designing of the garments.

# Company identity and branding

A designer or company can put a great deal of money, time and expertise into the development of new fashions or clothing innovations. When a product and a means of retailing it to a target market have been set up, the company will want to protect its product and give it a unique and recognizable identity.

All fashion companies like to have a **logo**, label or shop fascia (nameplate) to promote their wares and to encourage and reward the loyalty of their customers. Sometimes to be seen wearing a popular brand or label is more important to the consumer than the actual item of clothing. **Brand names**, **trademarks** and logos are registered for a fee, granting the firm exclusive usage. Trademarks can also be registered internationally. Companies can even register certain design features; Chanel, for example, has registered its signature quilted handbag with gilt chain, while Levi Strauss has registered the distinctive double-stitching on the back pockets of its jeans. Registration does not cost very much, and in time the brand or logo can become an asset in its own right, adding considerable value to quite simple garments such as T-shirts and underwear. Nike, which bought its logo from a young designer named Caroline Davidson for just $35, now pays out millions to promote and protect it – so precious is its commercial and symbolic power. Using a label falsely, or counterfeiting, is a prosecutable offence in the United States and to signatories of the EU Counterfeit Goods Regulation 1986.

## Copyright

In the domain of fashion it can sometimes be hard to determine the origin of a design. Very often new fashions evolve as improved versions of their predecessors. Some classic styles such as men's shirts, the six-panelled skirt and hipster flares are so commonplace that they are said to be in the public domain, and cannot be protected. However, from time to time there are innovations in the use of materials or cutting or a genuinely new arrangement of clothing features that represent a design worth protecting with copyright or a patent. The creator can register the design as his or her own, unless working for a company, in which case the company owns the rights of use, usually for life plus seventy years. The fashion designer can only register an original illustration of a design, not a finished garment. It must be signed, dated with a postmarked stamp, marked clearly with the copyright symbol and deposited with a bank or solicitor. Others must then ask for permission for a licence if they wish to use the design and pay a royalty on each garment produced. The industry standard is between 3 and 8 per cent of wholesale price. French couturier Pierre Cardin is the king of such licence agreements; in the 1970s he had over 800 licensees producing fashion, accessories and household items under his label. Poor-quality licensed goods may ultimately harm the company identity.

If copies are made illegally, copyright is said to have been infringed and the case may be taken to court. The copied garment is called a knock off. Unfortunately, copyright law stops at national boundaries. A design copyrighted in the United Kingdom is only protected within that country. Most pirating of clothing is done in the Far East. In Indonesia, the Philippines and Taiwan, intellectual property is not recognized and very little can be done about counterfeits. In the United States, in spite of well-established copyright law, there was a longstanding tradition of knocking off couture gowns as soon as they were imported to the top stores. Although couturiers granted rights to a few American manufacturers, these were widely abused and the trade took full advantage of the poor monitoring of such practices.

Counterfeiting can be difficult to prove; when is a fashion house following a trend, and when is it breaking the law? In cases where patterns have been stolen or copied from a contractor's factory, original garments found in pieces, or fabric printed up to order, the case is clear-cut. Many companies take strong measures to protect their intellectual property; others take the view that imitation is the sincerest form of flattery and move on quickly to new things.

For the budding designer, it is crucial to appreciate the difference between being influenced by the work of others and copying. While you are a student you are expected to study and research historical and contemporary clothing for cutting techniques and stylistic details and to draw and analyse the work of notable designers. To be inspired by others is natural. It is often said that there is nothing new; many designs reappear and get recycled. The truth is that the bona fide creative designers use modern fabrics, subtle differences in cut and fit, and the way that a style is worn with other items to update a look and create a new fashion. As a student you should place a high value on originality.

# The price cycle

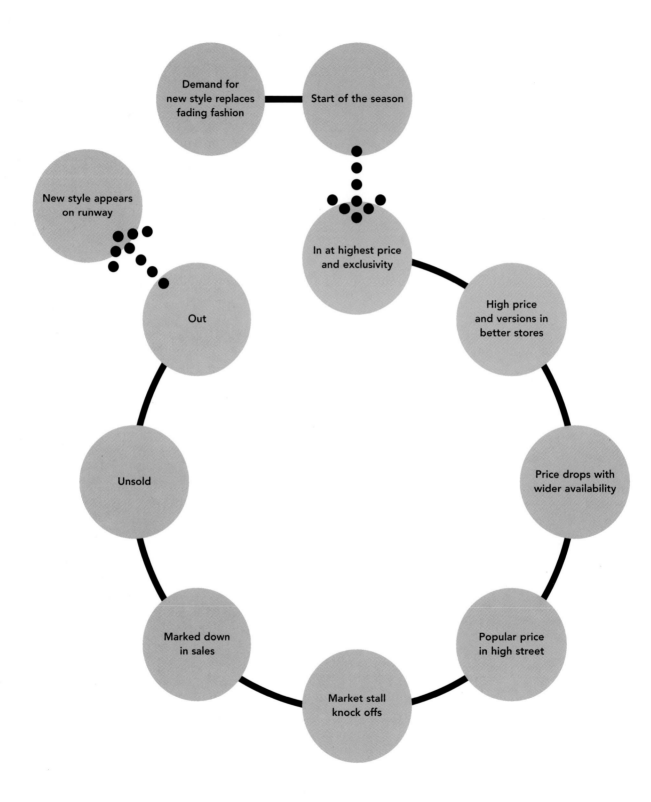

# The body III

# Inspiring bodies

We know from the earliest recorded examples that those responsible for making clothes were inspired by the body and its interaction with materials to create new, functional and decorative body coverings. In order for the coverings to be effective and comfortable and to stay in place, the designer needs an understanding of the mobile structure that is the human body. The evolution of clothing as we know it has taken many centuries. It has gone hand in glove with the ability to measure, map and illustrate the human form and communicate that information to others.

## Visualizing the body

To design fashion you need a solid understanding of anatomy – how the muscles are attached to the skeletal structure and how they work in movement with the frame. These are the underlying forms that will dictate how a fabric fits and moves in harmony or at variance with the body. The expression of attitude – frailty, solidity, energy or lassitude – depends on pose and elements such as the tilt of the head upon the spine or the point of a foot. The fashion designer needs to be able to visualize the body before working on a collection.

The physical structure of the body is symmetrical around a vertical axis. The head forms a central apex to a silhouette that is triangular whether seen from the front or sideways in motion. In everyday life we see and recognize bodies from many viewpoints and in movement; however, in visualizations of the body it is most commonly seen from the front and in a passive pose, with the upper body and face as the prime focus. The contours of the schematic male and female body are significantly different. The female form is more rounded in all dimensions, classically simplified and often exaggerated as the archetypal hourglass figure. The male body has a flat 'inverted triangle' silhouette with broader shoulders.

The more complex, rounded form of the mature female form is easier to draw but harder to dress: it provides a greater challenge for dressmakers. Women have suffered painfully through the centuries, corseting, hobbling and binding themselves to conform to the prevalent standards of sexual attraction. Sociologists and costume historians disagree about whether it is the male or the female who has driven the demand for clothing that flatters or emphasizes the figure and helps to attract a mate.

## Body beautiful

All societies form an idea of beauty. We constantly compare ourselves with each other from a young age; we objectify our own and others' bodies. These impressions are reinforced by collective opinion. Thinness and muscularity are seen as indicative of youth, an active life, self-control over the body and sexual ambiguity or freshness. Height literally implies superiority: the tall have to look down on others. The ideal is usually healthy and happy with well-groomed hair and with large, symmetrical facial features. However, throughout the last century there have also been significant trends towards using sickly, flat-chested and miserable-looking models. Twiggy epitomized the look of the underdeveloped, innocent and coltish adolescent that pervaded the plentiful 1960s and represented a paradoxical invitation to male protectiveness that ran counter to women's new-found freedom and financial independence. Her 'pale and interesting' look was the precursor of the waifish models of the 1990s.

**Below** The three basic body types: the ectomorph, mesomorph and endomorph.

**Opposite** The basic skeleton.

**Overleaf** Front and back views of the male and female bodies.

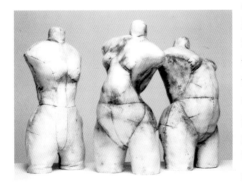

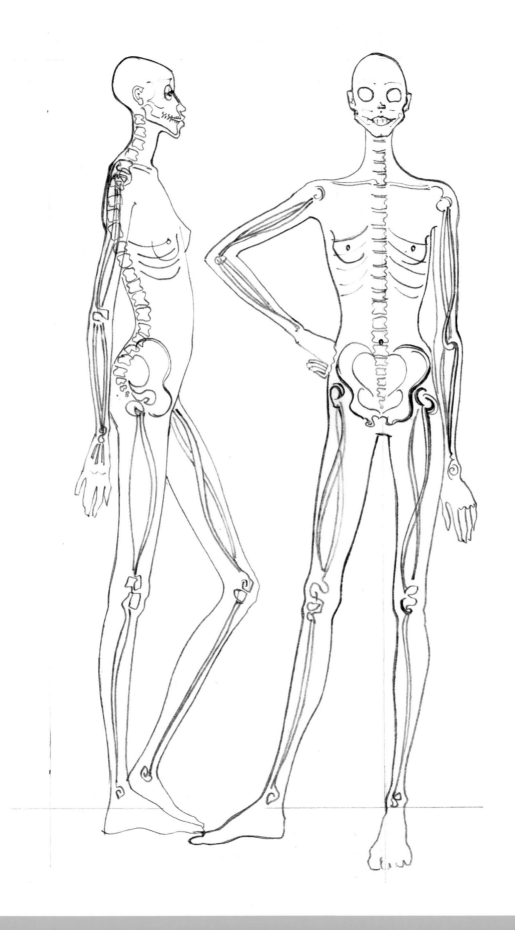

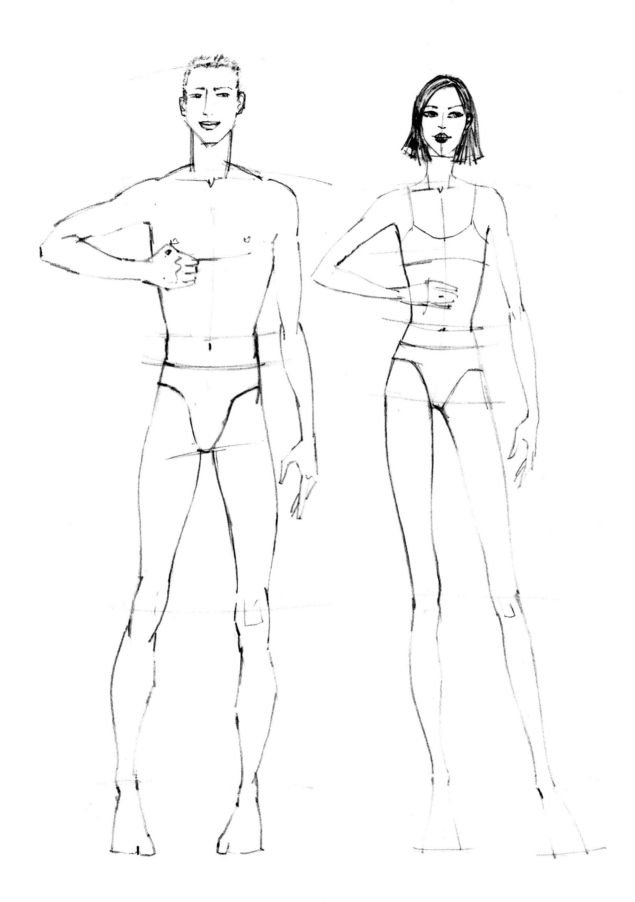

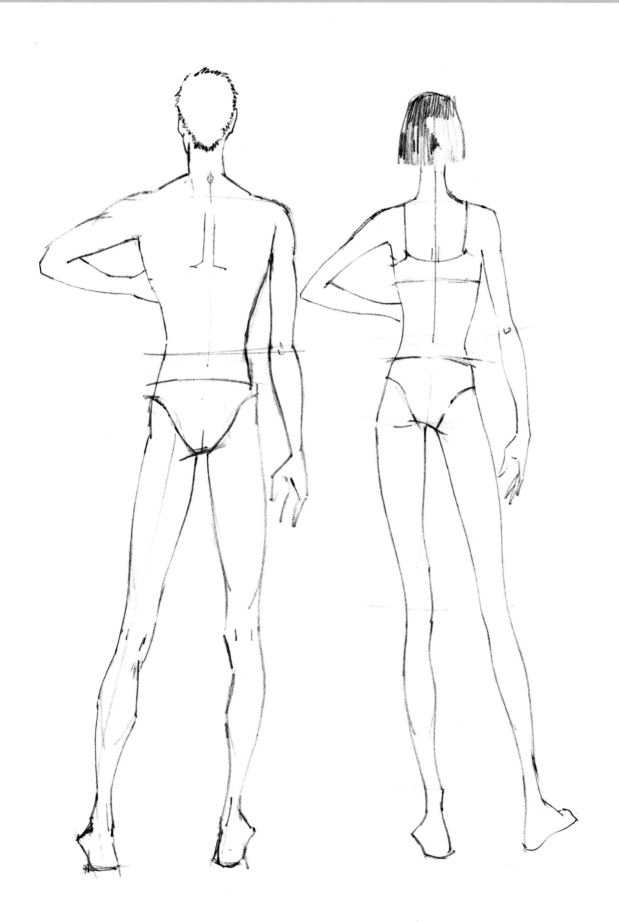

**Left** Since the 1960s, the Adel Rootstein company has been making display mannequins that epitomize the ideal body, attitude and look of the moment. The sophisticated, womanly look gives way periodically to the gauche adolescent.

**Below left** By clothing only the extremities of the body, you draw attention to the torso.

**Below centre** The hourglass shape of the model is emphasized by the contrasting panels on the dress.

**Below right** Today, the full range of ages and ethnic types is seen on the catwalk.

Until very recently fashion was a white, Western phenomenon, and black, Asian or oriental colouring was rarely seen in the media. However, today there is a greater presence of diverse and 'ethnic' models used on the high-fashion runways and billboards. They embody subtle but significant shifts in the aesthetics of physical form. Black models such as Iman and Naomi Campbell have paved the way for the African beauty Alek Wek.

Beauty, by its nature, is a rarity, so those selected by us are not representative of the masses. Less than 5 per cent of women have the dimensions of the fashion model. Today's model weighs 23 per cent less than the average person. Twenty years ago this figure was 8 per cent. We are so used to seeing painfully thin models in magazines and advertisements that people of average size consider themselves abnormal. We are unrealistic about the authentic appearance of the body. Many commentators blame the media and especially the fashion industry for this promotion of the unreal body. Indeed, many of the perfect bodies shown in the media do not actually exist; advertisers use digital technology to manipulate images of women to create impossible standards. Eyes and teeth are brightened, waists are whittled down, legs lengthened, and cellulite, wrinkles and blemishes airbrushed out.

## Emotion and gesture

Of equal importance as the visual and aesthetic appearance of the body is the attitude and appearance of the body in motion. While nude models have posed for paintings for centuries, the nature of the art enforced primarily still or languid postures. Posing for fashion photography has created a new language of gesture. A study of the work of photographers from Cecil Beaton to Juergen Teller, Rankin and Corinne Day reveals the importance of distinct attitudinal poses to each era. Internalizing these gestural exaggerations of the body, the fashion model learns to walk, swagger, pout and express a number of emotional states that can be read non-verbally. Madonna gave voice to this as 'Vogueing'. She reinvents herself and her body regularly with the happy complicity of fashion designers, notably Jean Paul Gaultier, who made fetishistic corsetry for her 1990 'Blonde Ambition' tour.

## The ideal

Designers, fashion stylists and photographers have often identified a model or personality as their inspiration or epitome of their ideal. They wish their clothes to be presented on the most desirable bodies of the moment, or to find some irresistible attitude that the model embodies. When a model goes for a casting for a fashion show she is asked to 'walk', to take a few paces, turn, pose and return, in a simulation of what will be expected of her on the runway. She may be asked to wear an outfit to see how it interacts with the body in movement. Fabric can behave very differently when worn – it can waft, rustle, bounce and drag, shimmer and dazzle.

What is required will vary with the designer, and perhaps with each collection. Some designers will want to see a confident, sexy swagger, others a slow, lethargic pace; a casualwear collection will demand a different attitude from an eveningwear range. If the collection accents a particular body part such as the back, the designer will want to see long, flawless backs. When Vivienne Westwood wanted to draw attention to the breasts and female curves, she found the voluptuous body of Sophie Dahl the perfect vehicle for her designs. Generally speaking, clothing

Kate Moss models Stella McCartney's designs. The choice of model is important to the delivery of the non-verbal message.

An illustration class using a live model.

hangs and drapes well from straight, broad shoulders. Long legs dramatize the shortness of a skirt or can carry a greater expanse of fabric in a long dress. Poses are emphasized by long limbs.

From time to time the designer may wish to express some other desirable attitude such as 'naturalness' or 'intelligence'. Issey Miyake has used men and women in their fifties and sixties to add *gravitas* to his collections. Alexander McQueen surprised the fashion world by championing Aimée Mullins – model, athlete and double amputee. He even designed a pair of hand-carved legs for her which she used to run at full speed down the catwalk.

# Drawing and illustration

As a fashion designer you must make decisions regarding the sort of body you are designing for: which features to emphasize, which to diminish and how much flesh to display. A sense of how fabrics drape and stretch across the figure can be learned by studying works of art and the history of fashion. But better still is first-hand observation of the figure and the trial and error of sketching, painting and rendering fabrics on a live model.

You can observe and draw people in almost any circumstances. Carry a small sketchbook with you and jot down silhouettes, lines and details that catch your eye. To signal the point of interest you should exaggerate rather than record faithfully. To some extent you will be inventing your ideal figure as well as the clothing. You can choose your own muse and illustrate your designs on that body, sketching the poses and attitudes that best express your designs. Yet it is imperative that you are aware that the fashion market does not exist for perfect bodies. Whatever their ideal, designers need the reality check of getting to know the human body and its interaction with fabric and clothing.

The fashion designer often needs to draw fast, to jot down a fleeting idea, to capture a transient movement, to proliferate enough ideas to edit into a coherent whole. Runway illustrators such as Gladys Perint Palmer and Colin Barnes have mastered the art of expressing shape, fabric quality and mood in a few dramatic lines more effectively than the camera.

> 'A lot of the time you're not really designing for "fashion people" but the general public who have some money to spend. People have hang-ups about their bodies so its no good doing that drapey one-shoulder thing; they are not going to wear it. You can't choose your customer; they choose you.' Designer Suzanne Clements

Fashion courses devote much time and teaching to life and fashion illustration classes, and a great deal of emphasis is placed on the ability to express ideas visually and originally. The fashion illustration in its many forms is a highly valued tool for communicating both technical and aesthetic information. Drawing and painting for fashion has its own special conventions which must be learned and practised until a degree of skill becomes natural. You will also be expected to evolve your own 'handwriting': the sort of marks you make, the body that you are designing for, and lastly, your garment designs.

**Left** Quick pencil and charcoal drawings help to capture line and the volume of drapery.

**Overleaf left** The body proportions of a fashion illustration are usually elongated through the neck and legs.

**Overleaf right** There are various pivot points used in fashion illustration that are emphasized to give attitude to the sketch.

## Life drawing

In life-drawing classes you have a first-hand opportunity to learn about anatomy and to observe how muscles and bones work together and balance one another in various movements and poses. Studying the life model will help you to draw shape and volume, and to use line and shade convincingly. You will be able to try out various different media, including soft pencils, pastels, paint and collage. You will find that some media suit your natural style and gestures more than others and that you prefer to work at a certain scale or on a particular sort of paper. Do not restrict yourself, and remain open to trying various approaches. Some people prefer neat, detailed line drawings; others use bold and expressive application of colour. The tutor in charge of the class may offer advice, suggesting, for example, that you try a different viewpoint, or a harder pencil on the outlines. There is no right or wrong way, however. You must find your own style.

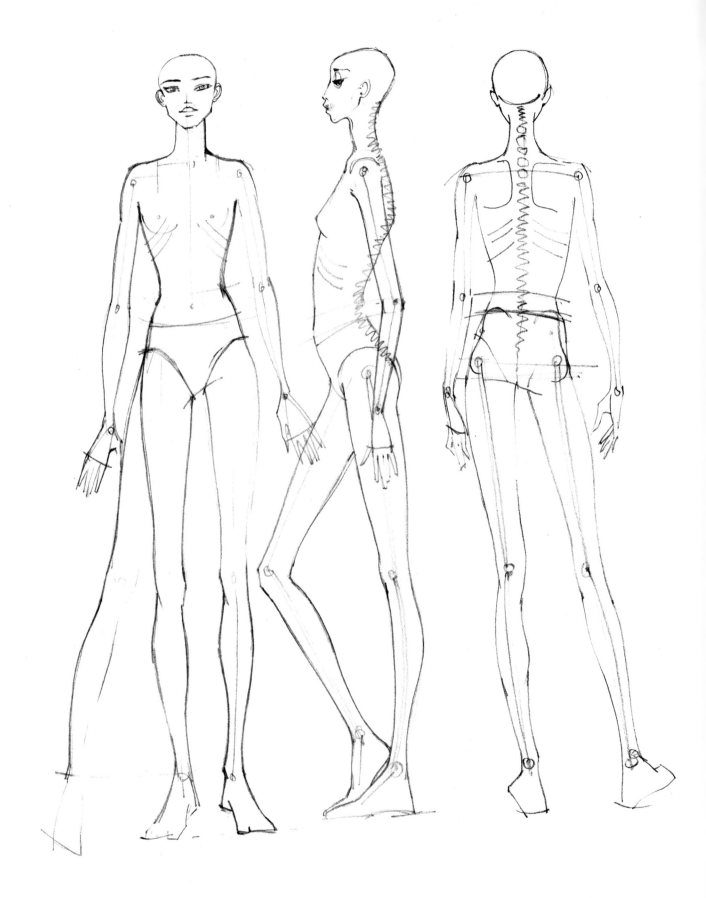

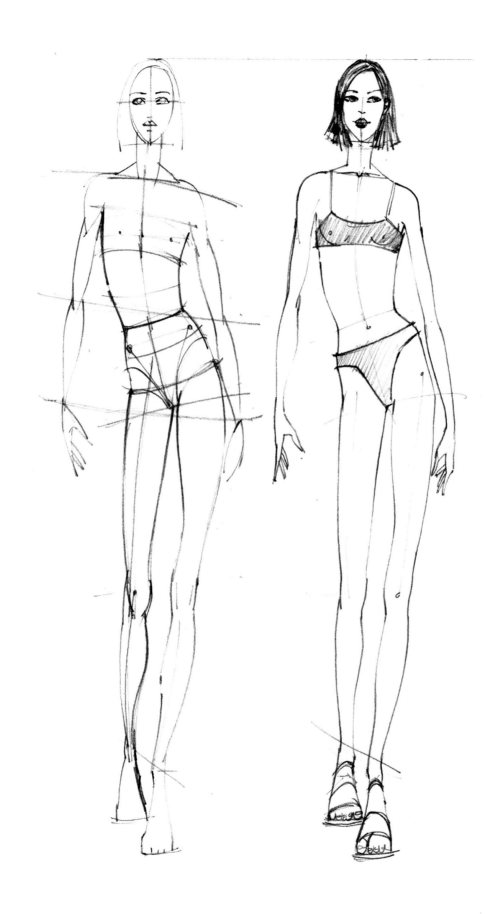

**Above** The tutor in charge of the illustration class offers advice and encouragement.

**Below right** This illustration captures a sense of frenetic movement. The butterflies and their wings are used in the collage to shimmer and indicate fabric ideas.

'Some students love to paint and draw, more than designing. It's not an academic thing; it's like playing, having fun, making a mess – it doesn't have to be realistic, you can express yourself on paper and let your own originality come through.' Illustrator and educator Howard Tanguy

In illustrating for fashion there are a number of significant differences of technique from ordinary life-drawing and painting that need to be taken into account and mastered. There are basically two different approaches to fashion illustration: free illustration and schematic drawing. When done with artistry and flair, fashion illustration has the magical ability to capture the intention and essence of a design and how it should be worn. To get it right there is no substitute for hard work and practice, not only to accurately render design ideas but also to hone your own style.

**Free illustration**
Free illustration is very similar to life drawing, and at college you will probably have timetabled fashion-illustration classes. The fashion sketch does not aim to capture a likeness but a mood or 'look'. Fashion models are notably taller and thinner than the average person and their bone structure is often apparent; attention therefore is given to those points where the bones show. Be aware of how a tilted axis, such as the pelvis, affects the stance and position of other parts of the body.

Body proportions are distorted, with heads drawn smaller and necks and legs longer than in the classical life drawing. In the average woman's body the head will divide into the height about seven-and-a-half times. For fashion drawings this increases to eight-and-a-half or nine times. The length of the legs is exaggerated more than the torso. Because the emphasis is on the clothing, the figure is elongated a little to allow more room for showing details such as pockets and seam lines, but not so much that the clothing would not work in reality.

The body is usually sketched standing and from the front in a relaxed pose. More dynamic poses are used for casual and sportswear. Three-quarter poses can be useful for showing side seaming or back details. If the back detailing of a garment is important or differs markedly from what might be imagined, a more lightly sketched back view is included. Arms are usually drawn away from the body rather than obscuring it; face, hands and feet are not shown in detail unless they are crucial to the design.

Simplification is a key element in fashion sketches; shading is not essential except to add depth to drapery or a sense of weight or emphasis to a silhouette. Buttons, zips and important details will be shown, but fabric texture or colour is not usually rendered all over a style but only marked here and there. Colour washes, tints and marker pens are often used to differentiate flesh tones and fabric. There are a number of shorthand marks that can be used to indicate folds, pleats and fabric types such as fur, knitwear and denim. Background and floor are often not indicated at all, or merely by a horizontal line, to stop the figure from looking as if it is floating.

Drawings are not laboured over; the objective is to communicate a particular line, feature or mood quickly and stylishly. Speed in drawing adds a certain spontaneity and confidence to the line. For this reason you will often be encouraged to draw quick poses and capture the key elements of a design.

For a talented few, fashion illustration will be their *métier*. For most professional designers, however, illustration will be used to make roughs, or design developments, and finished illustrations done only to show a line-up for a fashion presentation or give a journalist a preview of a coming collection. It is easy to become anxious and oversensitive about lacking talent in this area, when in fact the ability to make the clothing may be more relevant.

**Above** These drawings have a naive charm that reflects the girlish clothing designs.

**Below left** Students will practice drawing the body from many different views, exaggerating the angles to improve their sense of the three-dimensional form.

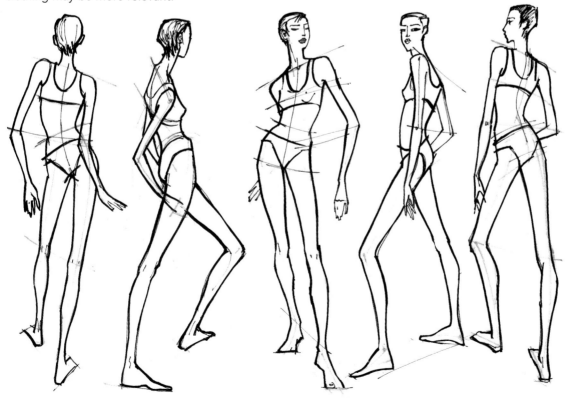

**Left** Paint and wet paper have been used here to give a languid look to the design.

**Opposite, above** Men's cargo pants; trouser flats should show the front fork and side seams, especially if there is top stitching. A bold outline gives emphasis to the drawing.

**Opposite, right** An 'animated flat' drawn with a thick felt pen and a fine drafting pen. Bending the arms and putting in some lines to indicate fabric folds makes the drawing a little more lively.

**Opposite, far right** A technical drawing, or spec, has measurements added and shows every detail in proportion.

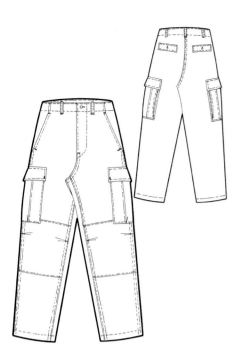

## Schematic drawing: specs and flats

Some students prefer to work with the schematic type of illustration, usually known as **specs** and **flats**. Specs and flats are the least ambiguous of fashion-illustration styles. These are working drawings of a garment that are done in a clear, diagrammatic manner to clarify technical detail. No body is drawn in a spec or flat. It is, however, essential to know what size of body the garment is intended to fit. In this instance it is important that there is no exaggeration of the proportion, and that every seam line, construction and trim detail is indicated by a flat, unshaded graphic to prevent mistakes happening in production. The industry finds this format easier to interpret than free illustration.

The conventions of drawing specs and flats are still developing and it is a style that integrates well with new technologies. It can be readily scanned and adjusted in a computer or faxed to suppliers and laser-cutting CAD/CAM machinery with no loss of detail. The essence of this form of fashion illustration is to communicate; it is an international language and is especially important in menswear, casualwear, sportswear and knitwear.

Flats are usually drawn by hand to an approximate scale, but the use of computer vector drawing programs (see page 74) allows more precision. For instance, the spacing and actual quantity of buttons would correspond to the correct dimensions to be used. Body, shoulder length, sleeve width, collar size and pocket size should all be proportionately correct. Top-stitching is indicated by a fine dotted line along the edge of a seam, which is drawn as a continuous line. Any complex detail may need to be shown as a zoomed-in enlargement alongside the flat. Colour can be used, and a little artistic licence is used to indicate softness of fabric, folds or even a 'ghost' body.

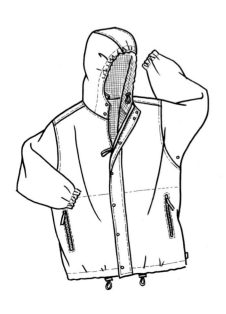

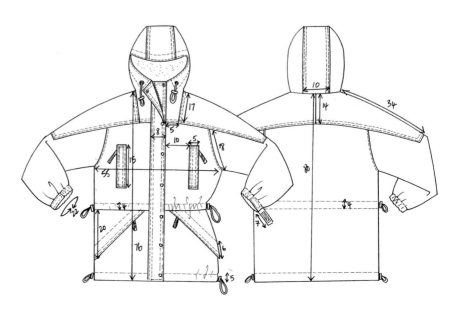

**Above left** These technical flats of shirts show the use of a striped fabric cut to chevron in the front and hidden yoke and cuff details.

**Above centre** Flats can be colour-coded to show fabric use.

**Above right** Knitwear flats use a shorthand technique to show stitch textures.

A spec (specification) is a more precise version of a flat and includes measurements and technical manufacturing details on the illustration or accompanying spec sheet which details trimmings, linings, threads and labels. Plain or squared (graph) paper can be used. When using squared paper, choose a suitable ratio of squares to centimetres (or inches), start with the grain lines and straight edges, and then add curves. It is a good idea to draw faintly in soft pencil and then go over the design with a drafting pen. Use a series of different nibs: for example 0.9 for outline, 0.7 for style lines and seams, 0.5 for top-stitching. When it is correct you can rub out the pencil. You can buy plastic templates for curves and shapes.

Flats and specs have a variety of uses: to accompany the cutting docket, in production processing and the sample room. Seamstresses prefer them to free illustrations as there is less margin for error. They are also used as salesmens' aids when selling collections and for keeping a visual archive of a range or line.

'I normally start my drawings on the back of a bus ticket and then I draw that up and then that is backed up by a proper spec drawing. I don't keep sketchbooks; I just have lots and lots of pieces of paper everywhere.'
Designer Joe Casely-Hayford

While you are at college you will be expected to do presentations consisting of finished illustrations. Fashion photographs and magazines are a good source of poses and are useful for analysing the way that folds and fastenings can be captured, but be careful not to trace or copy them directly. Students often arrange to pose for each other's drawings. The computer can also be a useful tool for illustration, not only for scanning in and transforming your hand-work but also for generating new styles and techniques that would be too laborious or impossible by other means.

# Using computers

Textile designers, graphic designers and illustrators have long been using the computer as a design tool. Until recently, however, the fashion designer has found it easier to create sketches and spec sheets by hand. Vast improvements in the quality, user-friendliness and price of computer systems and software for the fashion sector have gradually changed the relationship between the fashion designer and computers.

In the 1980s much of the computer hardware (and software) for the fashion industry was sold as stand-alone systems, often called **CAD/CAM** (Computer-Aided Design/Computer-Aided Manufacturing). These could not only organize and speed up the design process but could also work a piece of machinery such as a weaving loom or laser-cutting device. Often these units were unable to communicate with each other, and software had its own particular sort of interface and required special training. These systems are still very effective and are used in a great many fashion studios and manufacturing plants. You may find yourself using such a machine at college or on a work-experience placement.

Microsoft's Windows environment has become the standard by which most program software is operated. This, together with the growing availability of third-party programs or off-the-shelf applications, means that it is now possible for you to learn how to use the computer in a way that will be extremely useful to you in most workplaces.

The use of computers has brought with it a whole new lexicon of jargon and baffling acronyms. This language is not going to go away and it may be necessary for you to absorb at least a little of it so that you can communicate effectively with printers, manufacturers and graphic designers.

There are two distinct ways that the computer can deal with visual information: vectors and bitmaps. What follows is a technical explanation of each that will help you to choose the right approach for the task in hand.

The computer can be used to visualize garments on the body.

### Vectors

The most familiar form of computer illustration is technical drawings and specifications. They are necessary to the design process because they are less open to misinterpretation by the manufacturer than a sketch. The most effective way of doing this work on a computer is with a mathematical language called 'object-oriented vectors' or simply 'vectors'. The vector language PostScript, developed by Adobe, is ideal for drawing lines, curves and geometric shapes because it will always produce the sharpest, smoothest lines, with no jagged edges or blurs, that the computer monitor or printer is capable of, no matter what size the image is reduced or expanded to. Vector files are very economical on memory and will not degrade if resized. Patterns and specs can be transmitted across the world, downloaded very quickly and accurately zoomed up to size in this form.

Vector-based illustration takes a little practice but is proving to be a worthwhile creative as well as technical tool. Vector-based commercial programs such as Adobe Illustrator, CorelDRAW and Macromedia Freehand have introduced functions such as colour fills, gradients, text and text-wrapping, seamless pattern repeats and fills, customizable pens and media and hundreds of filters. It is possible to scan in hand-drawn work and convert it to a smooth vector drawing. The menswear sector of the industry is an especially keen user of vector-based illustration and specs. It is also used to make logos and patches for sports clothing and T-shirt design.

### Bitmaps

Bitmap, or raster-based, programs are best suited to realistic images such as photographs. A bitmap is a collection of dots of light, also known as pixels. Bitmapped images are resolution-sensitive, which means that the designer must decide before starting work at what scale he or she wants the finished result to be output. Work that is resized upwards can turn out to be very jagged or blurry looking, while reducing in size can result in loss of essential detail.

Bitmapped images have many advantages, however. Because each pixel can be edited or adjusted, they are good for refined details of tone and colour. Two-dimensional sketches, photographs and swatches can be scanned into the computer, saved as an image file, and then adjusted or combined. Small and fairly flat objects such as buttons, trimmings and yarns can also be scanned, scaled down and used in the artwork. Scanned line drawings can be useful templates to work over and, with the use of a printer, you can run off any number of flipped or rotated duplicates and variations. You can use magazine tearsheets of model poses and materials and accessories as a starting point for quick and effective collage design. Backgrounds can be cleaned up, and textures or exotic locations dropped into place.

> 'I've been illustrating for over twenty-five years and I've always said I'd never use a computer, but now you can't tear me away from mine. There's so much less time wasted on redoing things if the client wants it changed, and you can still charge the same. It's been worth every penny. The big breakthrough was the digitizing pen and tablet – just like using a felt pen or brush.' Fashion illustrator Neil Greer

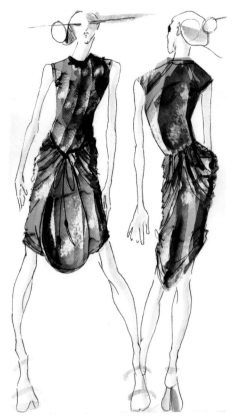

Many designers use a mouse or the more responsive graphics tablet with a pressure-sensitive pen to draw and paint directly into the computer. The effect is as intuitive as illustrating by hand without the mess or the multiplicity of materials needed in the studio. There is no waste, no dried-up inks and paints and no further outlay on painting materials. There is also no need to lug around a large box of art materials every day.

## Other uses

As a design range grows, the computer can be used to collage the storyboards from day to day. This is especially useful if you are working in a team. The stages can be kept and shown as progress reports and the final artwork used as part of a marketing presentation. Three-dimensional objects and photographs of garments, in stages of production or as finished styles, can be input instantly with a digital camera. Some designers use this technique as an aspect of research and the design process.

As you become more sophisticated at manipulating the potential of the computer, you will have more control over how your work is presented. Not only can fashion marketing or promotion students put together magazine-quality layouts using desktop publishing (DTP) packages, but they can also mount slide presentations. Here the integration of headlines and fashion promotional text, even sound, can make a dynamic and powerful visual message. Web-editing tools can be used to generate not only websites but also interactive stories and video presentations utilizing catwalk or model footage that can be stored on removable media and sent to potential publishers or clients.

The virtual catwalk is not far off. It is already possible to generate 3-D models, fully clothed, walking and talking in your own creations. Some students will consider a career in the newer areas of video and sound editing for fashion. In future, most fashion students and freelance designers will find it useful at least to have the skills to produce a digital portfolio and curriculum vitae (résumé) to leave with potential employers to keep on file.

**Opposite** Vector graphics give a clean and sharp look to illustrations.

**Above** These illustrations use a combination of scanned artwork and computer-collaged and manipulated images as fabric ideas.

# The elements of design

Designing is a matter of mixing known elements in new and exciting ways in order to create fresh combinations and products. The main elements of fashion design are silhouette, line and texture. The ways in which these elements can be used are called principles; they are repetition, rhythm, graduation, radiation, contrast, harmony, balance and proportion. Use of these variants causes a response – sometimes strong, sometimes subliminal – in the viewer or wearer. Understanding and controlling this response is essential to good designing. It is not always clear why a design works or not. At times the response can even be one of distaste or shock. However, the element of shock can also be positive in fashion terms.

The ability to articulate and analyse what is happening with a garment allows correction, amplification and development of the design. While a great deal of exciting design occurs through happy accident, it is an enormous advantage to be able to reflect on the effect of your work, to explain what is intentional and to gauge how close you are to achieving your desired result. An awareness of the elements and principles of design will also help you to evaluate other designers' strengths and to spot trends and changes in the market.

Some colleges will teach the elements and principles in a formal way; others will bring them into some project work or allow you to discover and experiment with them yourself without instruction. Good sources of information are listed at the end of the book.

## Silhouette

Garments are three-dimensional, and while we may think of the overall outline and shape of the worn garment as its silhouette, this silhouette changes as the garment is viewed in 360 degrees – moving, bending and revealing its volume. (In the United States designers even call silhouettes 'bodies'.) Silhouette is almost always the first impact of a garment, as seen from a distance and before the details can be discerned. A collection should not have too many variations on silhouette as this tends to dilute the overall impact and weaken the message. Accentuating the female body with a waistline divides the silhouette into upper and lower shapes, which need to balance visually and proportionally for a harmonious effect.

Closely allied to silhouette is volume. The fullness and bulk, or lack of it, in a fashion style is usually visible in the silhouette. Garments can also have qualities of lightness or weight due to the use of heavy, padded or diaphanous fabrics. The viability of such styles is related to the contemporary idealized female form.

At certain times in history, clothing has taken on dramatic qualities of silhouette. During the fifteenth century, married women wore dresses with a high waistline and large amounts of fabric gathered under the bosom to increase the size of the stomach and therefore give an illusion of pregnancy and fertility. The pannier and farthingale dresses of the 1720s were flat and extremely wide, so much so that it was difficult for women to walk through doorways or pass each other in the street. In 1947, in the aftermath of World War II, Christian Dior shocked the world with his 'New Look', a collection that reintroduced the nipped-in waist and full skirt to women's fashion after the austerity and fabric rations of wartime. Since the 1920s, women's legs have been increasingly revealed by fashion; hemlines reached as high as the crotch in the 1960s and necessitated the invention of tights (or

*A range of dress shapes: Sheath, Shift, A-line, Tent, Empire, Fit and flare, Princess line.*

pantyhose) and a whole new market genre. The visibility of legs and the adoption by women of trousers added to the rich potential of the female silhouette.

## Line

We respond in different emotional and psychological ways to the variety of lines that are used in design. A line can be hard or soft, implying rigidity or flexibility. It can move in various directions, leading the viewer to look across, up, down or in a sweep around the body. It can emphasize or disguise other features. It can create illusions of narrowness or fullness. The most common use of line in fashion is in the seaming of the pattern pieces and in fastenings. Vertical seam lines create an effect of length and elegance because they lead the eye up and down the body. Horizontal lines tend to be shorter in span and therefore draw attention to the width of the body. Lines across the body can make the figure appear shorter and wider. In **bias** cutting, the seam lines travel diagonally across and around the body to give a flowing and dynamic quality to a fabric. Lines can also converge and diverge to give strong directional effects. Curved lines add a certain fullness and femininity to a garment and are often used to minimize waists and draw attention to the bust and hips. Balancing the effects of design lines is one of the first tasks that you will tackle in designing through drawing and sketching your ideas.

## Texture

The fabric or materials that a garment is made up of can make or break a style that otherwise looks fine on paper or in toile form. It is both the visual and the sensual element of fashion design. In fact, most designers select fabrics before they make their design sketches. They prefer to be inspired by the texture and handle of a material than to find the perfect fit for a design sketch. A designer needs experience in how fabric behaves. Fabric is selected for its compatibility with the season, desired line and silhouette, price for the target market and colour. Colour can often be adjusted at a later stage in the process of range building by changing dye specifications, but the texture and properties of the fabric will remain constant.

# Silhouettes

Straight column

Natural

Trapeze

Hourglass

Egg shape

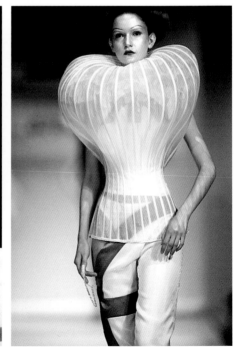

Shoulder wedge

# Line

The broad edge line emphasizes the size of this coat

Breaking all the rules for vertical and horizontal lines

A long, lean line with graphic effect

# Texture

A crisp cotton trouser suit

Soft knitwear for menswear

Soft mohair and masonry nails make a startling contrast of textures

Clothing is not just a visual but a sensory experience. It is essential to feel fabric and test it for its properties and associated uses. Fabrics with depth, rough surfaces and insulating qualities will be needed in cold weather, whereas smooth, flat or absorbent textures are more suited to summer. Different textures are required for various garment types: tailored suits and coats demand firm, crisp, hard-wearing fabrics which will show up sharp details such as collars and jetted pockets. Country and leisure clothing call for rougher-textured materials and warm, comfortable handling properties as well as easy care. Evening dress utilizes light, fluid, seductive fabrics that invite touch and can take gathers and embellishments well, such as jersey, satin, crêpe and chiffon (see also Chapter IV). We combine fabrics in the outfits that we wear, and designers working on separates will need an appreciation of good combinations of textures: bottom weights (skirts and trousers) and top weights (blouses). Contrasts of textures emphasize the difference between the garments and add allure.

Start collecting samples of fabrics in a notebook. Find out fabric names and weights and try them out in different combinations. Observe how professional designers use fabric combinations. It is also useful to learn how to describe the textures of fabrics verbally. The language of fabrics is rather like that of wine-tasting; it means little to the outsider but can be invaluable when discussing fabric with a supplier.

# The principles of design

The principles of fashion design are not always taught, discussed in crits or consciously employed, but they exist nonetheless. They are an important part of the aesthetic toolkit and are the means by which designers can subtly adjust the focus and effect of designs. Knowing where to find them and change them helps you to view designs objectively. They are usually the key to why a design does or doesn't work. Deliberately flouting these principles is as valid as using them with care if it gets the message across.

### Repetition

Repetition is the use of design elements, details or trimmings more than once in a garment. A feature can be repeated regularly or irregularly. This multiple effect can be used to unify a design. Some examples of repetition, such as evenly spaced buttons, are so common a feature that we tend not to notice them until we see an irregular version. The human body is symmetrical, so some repetition is inevitable in the mirroring of one side with another.

Repetition can be a part of the structure of a garment, such as the pleats or panels of a skirt, or a feature of the fabric itself, such as a striped or repeat-printed fabric or applied trimmings. From time to time asymmetrical garments such as single-sleeved tops or skirts that are longer on one side come into vogue as a reaction to the natural rule. Breaking the repeat has a jarring and eye-catching effect.

### Rhythm

As in music, rhythm can create a powerful effect, whether it comes through the repetition of regular features or through motifs in printed fabrics.

Changing the placement of colour in an outfit alters our perception of the figure.

## Graduation

This is a more complex type of repetition where features of the garment are worked in increasing or diminishing sizes or steps. For example, sequins on an evening dress can be heavily encrusted at the hem but fade in number as they travel up the garment. Gathers could be full in the centre of a yoke, diminishing towards the sides. The eye tracks the different degrees of change through the design, so graduation can be used as a way of drawing attention towards or disguising body features.

## Radiation

Radiation is the use of design lines that fan out from a pivotal point. A sunray-pleated skirt is a good example of this, but it can be more subtly deployed in draped garments.

## Contrast

Contrast is one of the most useful design principles, causing the eye to re-evaluate the importance of one area of focus against another. It relieves the dullness of an all-over effect, such as a dress being worn with a contrasting belt. Colours draw attention to themselves and to the features and details that they frame. Placement of contrasting features requires care as they become a focal point. Contrasts in fabric texture heighten the effect of each material, for example a tweed jacket worn with a silk blouse. Contrasts need not be extreme; we talk of 'subtle contrast' in effect between wearing a suit with flat shoes or high heels.

## Harmony

Harmony is not quite the opposite of contrast, but it does imply similarity rather than difference: hues that do not clash, fabrics that blend well. Soft fabrics and rounded forms better lend themselves to harmonious design than sharp cutting or pressed garments. Italian fashion is renowned for its harmonious use of soft fabrics and colour mixed with organic and unaggressive tailoring. A collection that is harmonious is easy to mix and match and generally sells itself without advice from the salesperson.

# The principles of design

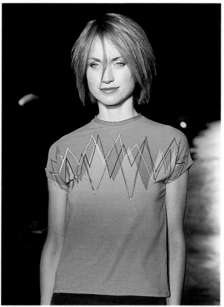

**Rhythm** The broken argyle pattern on this top gives it rhythm.

**Graduation** The buttons and collar graduate in size, adding interest to this shirt.

**Radiation** Ties radiate from a focal point on this parachute blouse.

**Repetition** Gathers on the neck and sleeve are a repeating principle.

**Contrast** A contrast between soft pink wool and hard metal fastenings.

**Harmony** A rounded top harmonizes with a straight skirt for a subtle and elegant look.

**Balance** Asymmetry demonstrated in a unique handmade felt top.

**Proportion** Playing with proportions can feminize a masculine look.

## Balance

The body is symmetrical through the vertical axis, and there is a tendency for our eyes and brains to want to keep it that way. We therefore look for balance in clothing. Vertical balance is our wish to see features mirrored from left to right: matching lapels, aligned and equal-sized pockets, evenly spaced buttons. Horizontal balance is affected when we say that an outfit looks top-heavy if all the emphasis is on the neck, or bottom-heavy if a skirt is too large or flouncy. The focus of an asymmetrical design often requires a smaller detail somewhere else on the outfit to echo and balance it. We look at a garment not just from the front and back, but also from other views. All aspects must satisfy the principle of balance or say something to us about their lack of respect for order, as in postmodern Japanese and Belgian fashion.

## Proportion

So much has been written about proportion in the realms of art, architecture and design that it seems almost pretentious to apply it to fashion as a rule or tool for achieving effects. However, the same principles apply and are subtle in their power to make or break a design. Proportion is the way we visually relate all the separate parts to the whole. It is done by measuring – not necessarily with a tape measure but with the eye. We can create illusions of body shape by changing the proportions of design features or by moving seams and details around.

The positioning of horizontal hemlines has a dramatic effect on the proportions of the body.

# Bodice, neckline and sleeve shapes

The front bodice can be made to fit in many different ways through manipulation and suppression of fabric during the pattern development.

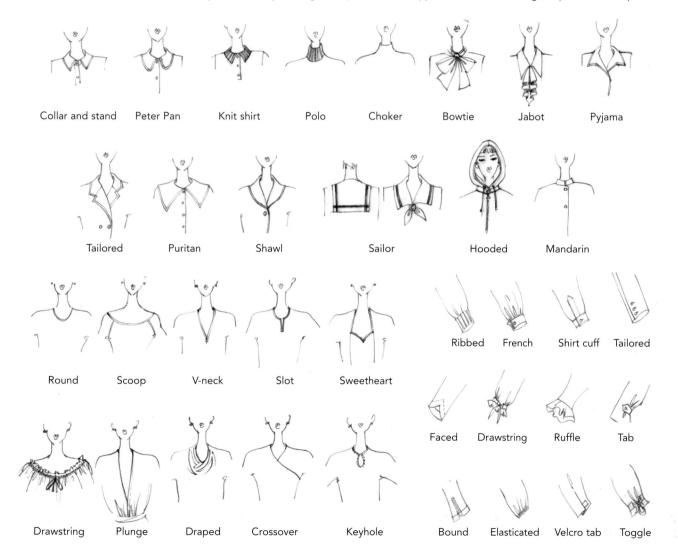

| Collar and stand | Peter Pan | Knit shirt | Polo | Choker | Bowtie | Jabot | Pyjama |

| Tailored | Puritan | Shawl | Sailor | Hooded | Mandarin |

| Round | Scoop | V-neck | Slot | Sweetheart |

| Ribbed | French | Shirt cuff | Tailored |

| Drawstring | Plunge | Draped | Crossover | Keyhole |

| Faced | Drawstring | Ruffle | Tab |

| Bound | Elasticated | Velcro tab | Toggle |

# Skirt and trouser shapes

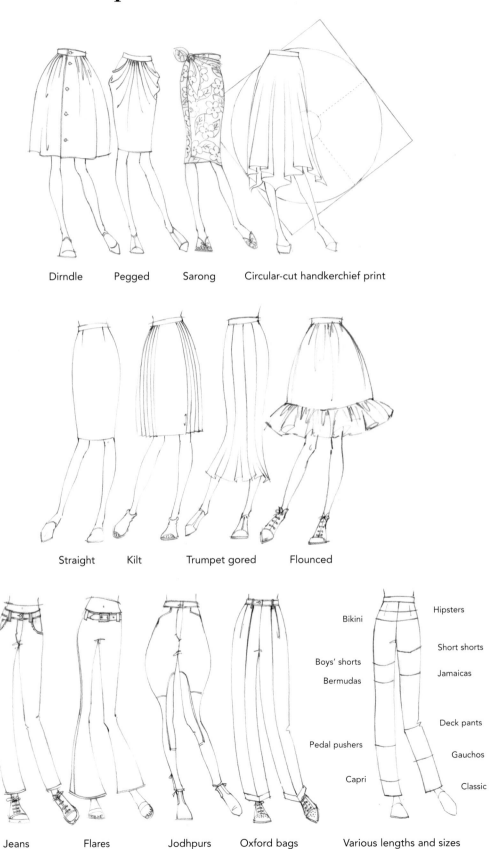

Dirndle    Pegged    Sarong    Circular-cut handkerchief print

Straight    Kilt    Trumpet gored    Flounced

Bikini    Hipsters

Boys' shorts    Short shorts

Bermudas    Jamaicas

Pedal pushers    Deck pants

Gauchos

Capri    Classic

Jeans    Flares    Jodhpurs    Oxford bags    Various lengths and sizes

# Colour and fabric IV

# Colour basics

Research carried out by yarn, textile and garment manufacturers and retailers indicates that the consumer's first response is to colour. This is followed by an interest in the design and feel of the garment and then an appraisal of the price. Choosing colours, or a **palette**, for a fashion range is one of the earliest decisions to make when designing a collection. The colour choices will dictate the mood or seasonal 'tune' of a collection and help to differentiate it from its predecessor.

People respond intuitively, emotionally and even physically to colour. Blues and greens – the colours of sky and grass – have been shown to lower blood pressure, while red and other intense colours can speed up the heart rate. White can make you feel cold; yellow is a sunny, friendly colour; grey can be businesslike or depressing. The 'little black dress' denotes sophistication and elegance, while the little red dress symbolizes fun and sexiness. People brought up in an urban setting will respond to a different palette to those from rural or tropical communities. The same colours can look different or inappropriate in various settings or lighting conditions, for example, in cloudy daylight or under fluorescent shop lighting. Dye technologists recognize this and recommend different intensities of dye and **light fastness** for, say, Manchester, Miami and Bombay.

'Pink is the navy blue of India.' Diana Vreeland, editor of American *Vogue* from 1963 to 1971

The seasons and climate will account for some colour choices. In autumn and winter people are drawn to warm and cheering colours or to dark colours to help retain body heat. Conversely, white (which reflects heat) and pastels are worn more often in spring and summer. There are many social conventions and symbolic meanings attached to colours; in parts of the West it is widely believed that green is unlucky, yet it is also associated with nature and wholesomeness. In India, scarlet, not white, is the colour associated with weddings. In China, white, rather than black, is the colour of mourning. When designing a collection, it is important to take into account the context of the target market.

## Defining colours

The average human eye can distinguish some 350,000 different colours, but we do not have names for all of them. In attempting to describe a colour we approximate in the hope that others will see the colour in the same way. A number of systems have evolved that try to identify and define colour scientifically. The first was devised by the English physicist Sir Isaac Newton in 1666, when he discovered that all colours were present in natural light and could be separated by passing light through a prism. He identified the colours of the spectrum – the seven prismatic colours – red, orange, yellow, green, blue, indigo and violet. He also believed that these seven colours could be related to the musical scale, suggesting colour 'tones' and 'harmonies', and since then colour has often been discussed in musical terms. Newton also constructed a six-spoke colour wheel (indigo and blue were merged), which is still used to describe pigments and subtractive colour today. In 1730, Jacques-Christophe Le Blon discovered that mixing two of the primary colours – red, yellow and blue – created the secondary colours – orange, green

and violet – and, in different ratios, other intermediate hues. Mixing all the primary colours created the tertiary colours: various shades of brown and grey, all the way to black.

Besides naming the colour itself, we describe its characteristics through the three dimensions of hue, value and intensity. Hue refers to the basic colour, such as blue, red or green. There are relatively few pure hues. Value refers to the lightness or darkness of a colour varied on a scale of white (the sum and source of all colours) to black (the total absence of light). Lighter values are called tints, the darker ones shades. Intensity is the relative strength (purity) or weakness (impurity) of a colour. Diluting a pigment with water will lower its intensity; for example, red becomes rosy pink and then pale pink.

**Above, from left to right**
The little black dress is always in fashion.
A black-and-white contrast looks chic and fresh.
White can look starkly clinical and dramatic.

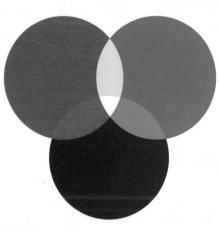 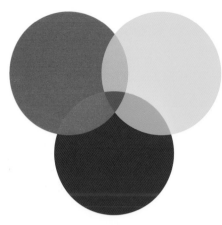 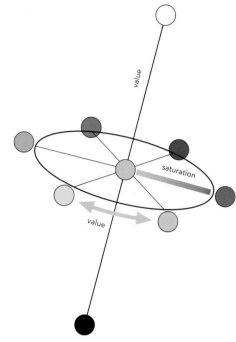

### Additive colour

System of mixing physical primaries (light). When projected in combination, red, blue and green produce white light.

### Subtractive colour

Mixing the pigments red, yellow and blue creates the secondary colours: orange, green and violet

### Spectrum

Full range of colour, from violet to red, as produced by shining white light through a prism.

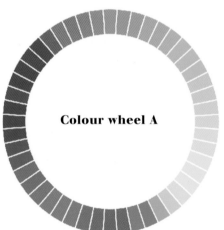 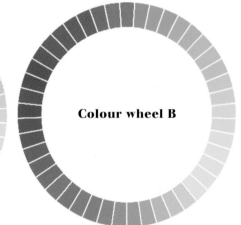

**Colour wheel A**

**Colour wheel B**

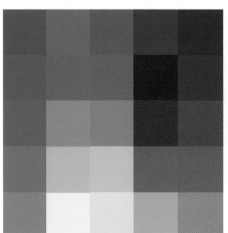 

**Simultaneous contrast** characterizes colour as a strongly relative phenomenon; colours change their appearance depending on their context.

In any colour scheme, as important as the identity of a particular colour is the relationship it shares with the other colours in the composition. A dull colour can be brightened, a strong colour can be subdued, an individual colour can change its identity in many ways, depending on the colours with which it is surrounded.

## Primary colours

Red, yellow and blue cannot be made by mixing other colours.

## Complementary colours

Colours, such as red-green, blue-orange, yellow-violet, which are optically opposed; they appear opposite each other on the colour wheel.

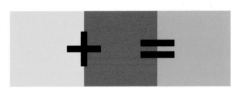

## Secondary colours

Orange, green, violet – colours made by mixing two primary colours. Yellow and red make orange, etc.

## Analogous colours

Those colours with a common hue which are adjacent on the colour wheel, eg blue-violet, violet and red-violet, etc.

## Value

That attribute which measures variation among greys, refers to the lightness and darkness of a colour.

Any hue can vary in value – red can become light pink or dark maroon.

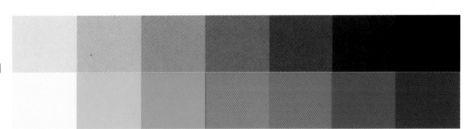

## Vibrating colour

Complementary colours of equal value, when placed together they cause a visual intensity exceeding their actual intensity, also known as simultaneous contrast.

A single colour makes a strong statement.

## Colour terms

Below are some common terms used by the dye and fashion industry to differentiate and combine colours.

*Tone* A 'greyed' colour.

*Deep* Rich, dark.

*Concentrated* Intense, saturated colour.

*Pastel* A colour tinted with white.

*Warm colours* Associated with fire, sunlight, passion (eg, red, orange, yellow, purple).

*Cool colours* Associated with sky, sea, ice, peace (eg, blues, violets, tints with white).

*Neutrals* Colours based on the tertiaries (beige, grey, brown, khaki, olive).

*Subdued colours* Colours shaded up or down by the addition of black, white, grey or a complementary colour (eg, yellow with a touch of violet creates dark gold).

*Monochromes* The gamut, or scale, of shades using a single hue from black to white.

*Ground colour* The dominant background hue, shade or tone.

*Accent colour* Colour used in a small proportion but which has a strong visual attraction.

*Harmonies* Two or more colours that look balanced and pleasing together.

*Contrasts* Colours that strongly emphasize their differences when placed next to each other; often they are directly opposing hues on the colour wheel (eg blue and orange).

*Complements* Almost opposing colour hues; they are more harmonious pairings than contrasts as they use a warm tone with a cool one.

*Analogous colours* Tints and tones that are close neighbours on the colour wheel.

*Subtractive colours* Colours mixed using pigments and dyes.

*Additive colours* Colours mixed using light or light absorption.

*Optical mixes* Iridescent colours that occur when two different colours are knitted or woven together, usually as warp and weft, so that, viewed from different angles, the fabric appears to change colour subtly. Optical mixes are used in jersey marls, cotton chambré and shot silks.

*Fugitive colour* Colour that washes out or bleeds (ie, is not fast).

*Simultaneous contrast* Effect occurring when the intensity of a colour appears to change based on the value of its background, or within a set of colours; often seen in stripes and prints and also in contrasts between skin tones and clothing.

Scientific descriptions of colour, however, cannot fully communicate the sensation or emotional effect of a colour, so we also name colours based on our familiar and shared knowledge of the world – after animals (for example, elephant grey and canary yellow); flowers and vegetables (lilac, mushroom, tomato red); sweets and spices (toffee, saffron); minerals and jewels (pearl, coral, jade) and so on.

This associative use of colour is helpful to remember colour shades and to name a palette, but it is not sufficient to indicate to a specialist the exact tone that is required for a match. In order to do this, a number of standardized commercial colour-matching systems have been developed. The most widely used in fashion

**Left** A sophisticated palette using iridescent analogous colours.

**Top** Layered pastels give this outfit a festive look.

**Above** Metallic colours such as gold and silver add glamour to a sheer fabric.

and textiles are the Munsell Colour System and the Pantone Professional Colour System. The Pantone method precisely calibrates a six-digit number to indicate the location of the colour on the colour wheel (first two digits) and compares its value to black and white (second two digits) and its intensity (final two digits). The Pantone system is included in many computer design software packages. Using this system, it is possible to ask a printer or dyer to reproduce your artwork to an exact specification.

## Colour forecasting

Colour prediction has become big business. It impacts not only upon clothing but also cosmetics, home furnishings, lifestyle products and the automotive industry. Dye companies cannot afford to make expensive mistakes, and must be ready to supply the demand for a colour up to two years in advance of the retail sale season. Colour forecasters for the fashion industry collate information from all over the world on sales figures and changes in market interest in colours. They then come together twice a year for conferences in Europe and the United States to summarize and define the broad industry trends.

The principal colour advisory bodies are the British Textile Colour Group, the International Colour Authority (ICA), the Color Association of the United States (CAUS) and the Color Marketing Group (CMG). In the process of analysing data, the forecasters also observe and interpret the underlying social and cultural context and make projections for the future. This informs the likely direction that colours in fashion may take. For example, during the 1990s many consumers were aware and concerned about the damage that chemical dyes were causing to the environment. Colour forecasters warned the dye companies to concentrate on more natural shades and formulations. This provoked a return to the use of softer-coloured 'natural' dyes and to the prevalence of undyed and unbleached materials in fashion.

'Every season I ask myself: What am I sick of the sight of? What have I seen out the corner of my eye? Like: lime green's a bit out now but watch out for pink for blokes.' Colour guru Sandy MacLennan

## Colour and the designer

Unless you work within a company where a large volume of goods in production means that you can order the dyeing of colours to your own palette, you will probably be restricted to colours that are offered by the fabric mills. These are usually the classical popular colours – variations of black, white, navy and red – and the fashion colours as predicted by the colour gurus and interpreted by the dye houses. It may take between six and eighteen months before the colours you choose at a fabric fair appear as a coordinated colour story in the shops.

While you are studying you should collect snippets of fabrics and pieces of paper in colours that appeal to you and start to build up your own colour library as reference material. This will help you to understand which colours form natural and pleasing combinations and how to balance the use of ground colours with accent colours. You may have access to a dye laboratory where you can experiment with dyeing shades in tones and making combinations to build up your own colour palettes.

Many colleges have a dye laboratory where you are encouraged to experiment with colour and printing techniques.

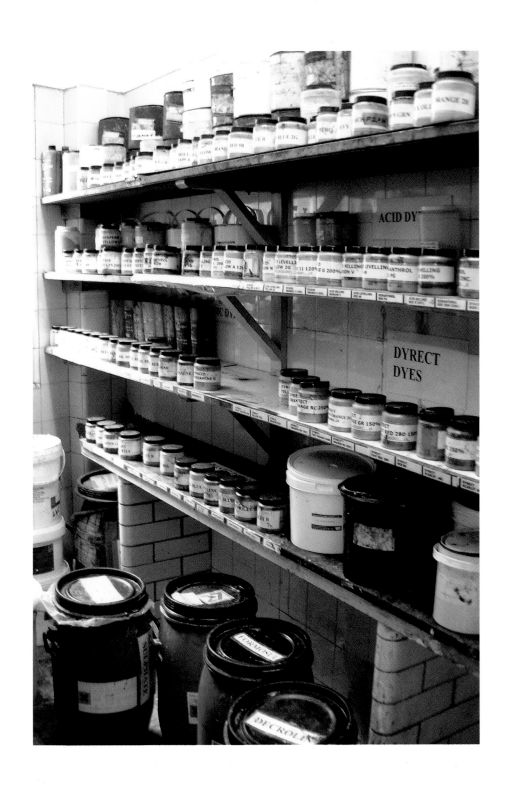

# Fabrics

Fabric is to the fashion designer what paint is to the artist: the medium of creative expression. Some designers work directly with the fabric, others might draw out ideas on paper and then search for an appropriate material. Choosing suitable fabrics is the key to successful designing. It is not only a matter of what one likes visually but also weight and handle, price, availability, performance, quality and timing. The suitability of a fabric for a fashion design comes from a combination of yarn, construction, weight, texture, colour, handling and pattern or print, as well as additional performance factors such as warmth, stain-resistance and ease of care. The designer must have a reasonable expectation as to how a fabric will behave; a fabric cannot be forced into a style or shape that is not compatible with its characteristics, both practically and visually.

You need to build up a good working knowledge of the different categories of fabrics, their sources, price structures and their suitability for various uses. Keep a notebook specifically for this purpose. There are some organizations that can help students to source fabrics.

## Fibre

Fibre or yarn is the raw material out of which the textile is made. There are three main categories of fibres: animal (hairs), vegetable (cellulosic fibre) and mineral (synthetics). An experienced designer can often identify basic fibres by hand and sight. Today there are very many sophisticated blends and branded versions of man-made fibres. The length of the yarn fibre (known as the **staple**), the method of spinning it into a yarn and its diameter will all determine the characteristics of the cloth. Blends modify the inherent properties of the main fibre. For example: cotton and linen are absorbent and also crease badly, but when mixed with polyester they dry faster and can be ironed more smoothly.

All commercial garments must carry a fibre content label by law. The highest fibre content is listed first as a percentage of the total. A blend of 75 per cent cotton and 25 per cent polyester will be labelled as cotton/polyester. This is accompanied by a recommended care label. A labelling scheme based on a language of symbols called the International Textile Care Labelling Code is used in many countries.

Textile manufacturers will tell you what the fibre content and weight are if you are buying in bulk. However, if you are buying fabric at retail this information may not be available. It is helpful if you can find out the content, not only to help future identification, but especially if you have in mind a finish such as pleating or a purpose for which the fabric may not prove suitable. If you are unsure of the composition of a fabric, you can do some simple tests yourself or send the fabric to a laboratory.

## Fabric construction

The two main ways in which fibre is made into fabric are weaving and knitting. Textiles produced by other methods, such as felt, net, lace and bonded fabrics, are classified as non-wovens. It is very useful for the fashion designer to have an understanding of the basic structures of materials as it will indicate how they can be applied and finished. It is important to know how they will wear, stretch and behave when the garment is worn.

Woven fabrics are created by interlacing vertical yarns (the **warp**) with horizontal yarns (the **weft**) at right angles to each other. These threads are also

Fibrillated viscose; fibres can be brushed up after weaving to give a soft handle.

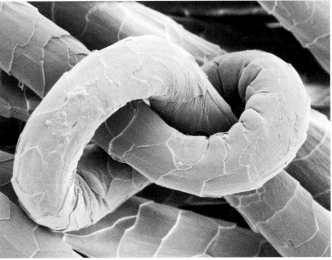

A knot in a wool fibre. The scales on a wool fibre open in warm soapy water and allow the fibres to lock together to make felt.

The knitted structure of a cotton jersey allows the fabric to stretch in both directions: width-wise and lengthwise.

Woven man-made polyester fibre in a plain weave.

A wool gabardine twill.

**Opposite, top and centre** This fabric has been handmade using a traditional patchwork technique called Suffolk puffs.

**Opposite, bottom** New qualities of yarn and fabric techniques are displayed at a Filasia trend forum.

referred to as the lengthwise or crosswise **grain** of the fabric. The tightness or set of a fabric is due to the number of warp and weft threads per inch or centimetre. The edges of the cloth are usually set with a higher number or stronger threads to stabilize the fabric. This is known as the **selvedge**. Because the warp is prestretched to weave evenly, most woven fabrics have good lengthwise stability. For this reason garments are usually cut out parallel to the selvedge so the body follows the lengthwise grain. The additional stretch of the crosswise grain helps the fabric stretch in places such as the seat, knees and elbows.

**Types of weave**

By changing the colour or yarn type in the warp and weft of the weave structure, an infinite variety of fabrics can be produced. In particular, the type of weave will make a difference to how the fabric drapes or behaves.

*Plain weave* The most common of all weave structures; when warp and weft are of the same size and closely woven, the plain weave is the strongest of all weaves. Fabrics made with a plain weave include calico, broadcloth, flannel, gingham and chiffon.

*Twill weave* Weave formed by the weft crossing at least two warp threads before going under one or more threads, producing a fabric with a diagonal surface pattern. Gabardine, drill and whipcord are popular twills. Herringbone is a variation that is used in suitings.

*Satin and sateen weaves* Weaves producing smooth, lustrous fabrics with high drape and a tendency to stretch. The threads are positioned with longer floats on the surface – on the warp surface in satin and the weft surface in sateen.

*Pile weave* Fancy weave using an extra filling thread that is drawn up and looped on the surface of the fabric. The loops can be left uncut, as in towelling, or cut or sheared as in corduroy, velvet and fake-fur fabrics. High-pile fabrics such as candlewick are made by a needle- or gun-tufting process applied to a woven backing.

*Jacquard weave* Intricate, figured weave produced on Jacquard loom. Each thread is programmed to lift or stay in place by a perforated card like a pianola roll. Brocade, damask and tapestry are Jacquard weaves used for eveningwear and special occasions.

Knitted fabrics are formed by linked loops of yarn. Horizontal rows are called courses, and vertical rows are called wales. They stretch in both directions and have a greater tendency to stretch crosswise. Their elasticity gives them good draping and crease-resistant properties, but by the same token they can also lose their shape with wear and washing. Because the structure is fairly open, knitted fabrics 'breathe' and can keep the body warm or cool, according to the choice of yarn. They are useful for underwear and active sportswear. As fine knits tend to cling to the body they are favoured for eveningwear. As with weaving, knitting can incorporate colour and pattern effects.

Most knitting constructions have been developed from the craft of hand-knitting. Today, modern machinery can produce fabrics and garments at high speed that are more complex than could be attempted by hand. A fully finished sweater can be made in forty-five minutes. Nevertheless, there is still a place for the unique qualities and charm of the hand-knitted garment in fashion. Machine-knitted fabrics vary from the sheerest of lingerie qualities to heavily cabled woollens. Machine-knitted fabric size is measured by gauge, abbreviated as 'gg'. This refers to the number of needles per inch or per centimetre.

## Types of knit

*Single jersey* In this knit, the face (the knit side) of the fabric is smooth, while the back (the purl side) is comparatively rough and therefore more absorbent. If a stitch is dropped or a hole made, the fabric will ladder or run down the length of the wale. Single jersey has a tendency to curl at the edges when cut. It is lightweight and ideal for T-shirts and lingerie.

*Double jersey* Also known as interlock, this uses a double row of needles to make a fabric that is smooth-faced on both sides, stable and less likely to bag or run.

*Ribbing* This is a vertical arrangement of needles knitting alternately purl and knit stitches to produce a stretchy, reversible construction. Ribbing is used to pull fabric close to the body at the waist, neck and cuffs and is also used with wovens as a trimming on sports clothing.

*Fair Isle* A single-jersey knit with small patterns using two colours of yarn at a time; developed from the sweater patterns of the Shetland Islands off Scotland. Jacquard Double-jersey patterned knitting using as many as four colours in a row; usually programmed and controlled by computerized machinery.

*Intarsia* Method of producing colourful single-jersey geometric and picture knits. More laborious than the Fair Isle or Jacquard methods, until the invention of computerized machinery it was confined to only the most expensive luxury and cashmere sweater markets.

*Warp knitting* A hybrid of knitting and weaving that uses a beam of warp threads linked together by a moving rack of needles. The created fabric will not unravel or run and is used for swimwear, sports clothing and lingerie.

The oldest method of making fabrics was by bonding or matting fibres together. When wool is moist, warm and pressed, the fibres interlock to form felt. This process has been extended to the production of thermoplastic man-made fused fabrics. There is no grain to these materials, they can be cut in any direction and do not fray or unravel. Some of the materials can be stretched and steam-moulded, as in rabbit-hair felt, to make hats. In the lingerie business thermoplastic knitted fabric that has 'memory' – that is, it returns to its desired shape after washing – is used for bra cups and the feet and calves of hosiery.

Supporting fabrics such as interfacings and interlinings that add body, shape retention and reinforcement at stress points are often made of bonded fabrics. These are commonly known by their trade names, for example, Staflex and Vilene. **Fusible** interlinings are coated with a glue to allow them to stick to the garment

**Opposite**  Very fine jersey drapes beautifully. Here the transparent layers create a changing moiré effect with every step that the model takes.

**Left**  Knitwear can be constructed in three dimensions directly on the machine without the need for seams. Here the technique is used to add drape to a heavy, soft wool.

**Top** Fabric mills and importers are keen to promote their new lines. Swatch cards are sent out to valued customers who may then order sample lengths or cuts to try.

**Above** Trade publications carry information about new products, market feedback and trends.

**Opposite** Trade show exhibitors interpret and forecast the prevailing mood in fashion.

fabric with heat pressing. Wadding is a high-loft fabric of puffed-up, matted fibres used in quilting and padding to give bulk or warmth to a garment.

Net and lace are fabrics made on complex machinery that allows threads to twist and travel diagonally. Lace fabric usually comes with a scalloped hem edge, and lengths are restricted to the width of the machine. Net and lace do not usually fray, but the open and rough surface quality of some lace demands that it is lined. Rubber and plastics are materials often used in the more esoteric fashion designs. Rubber is derived from the latex (sap) of the rubber tree and can be used in its liquid form and painted onto a mould or even directly onto the body. Rubber sheet can be cut and sewn or glued, and is available in translucent, solid colours, metallic finishes and prints. Plastics, polythenes and cellophanes have all been put to use in the fashion industry.

## Finishes

The textile industry is continually inventing new fabrics and processes. Tencel, Tactel, Sympatex, Supplex, Polartec, Aquatex, Viloft and Coolmax are all recent developments of synthetic materials. Many of the processes are applied after the fabric has been made and dyed and are known as finishes. Finishing can be for practical and performance improvement such as stabilizing, fireproofing and crease-resistance, or for embellishment and handle such as brushing, beading or embroidery. Finishes at first devised for the use of military, industrial or household

the tweens · we like jumping · running · colour · pets · shopping · music · sleepovers  1415  we are the net generation · we like cool · clubbing · kissing · technology · sex · drinking  2526  we are the flex generation · we love our kids · art · multi tasking  4041  we are the boomers · w

**Above** After a visit to a trade fair, the designer puts together fabric and colours to range-build and coordinate the sampled fabrics. Some fabrics will then be eliminated.

**Left** Yarn qualities and new colour palettes are developed and offered to the fashion wholesalers twice a year.

textiles are often used by the inventive designer for various sports or fashion garments. Companies patent these new processes and the proprietary trade names are used in the publicity and marketing of the fabrics.

Fabric printing has long been one of the most popular ways of finishing and decorating plain cloth, and there are many printing methods such as batik, heat-transfer (sublistatic) and screen printing that have their own distinctive looks. Add to this the many generic types of prints, such as florals, geometrics, abstracts, picture prints (known as conversationals) and other motifs, and the scope for design is infinite.

> 'Print, I think, you really have to fall in love with, it really is the most difficult decision to make. It can define the whole collection, but also you can see nothing else if it is too obvious.' Designer Sonja Nuttall

## Selection

As part of the initial research for a new season the designer will preview fabric and trimmings ranges. In some companies the designer will carry all the responsibility for fabric selection; in others the team will include a fabric merchandiser. A balanced range will include a variety of weights and textures, classic and fashion fabrics and sometimes prints or novelties. There will be a round of visits to trade fairs, mills and agencies to assess what is available. Textile companies will send out swatches and shade cards, and the designer will order sample lengths of fabric (cuts) to make trials.

When choosing fabrics for your design or collection you need to take account not only of the visual and technical properties of the materials supplied to you by the manufacturer but also the hand or handle. There is no substitute for feeling a fabric to assess its drape, surface qualities and weight. Selecting fabrics is an enjoyable part of designing, but it takes study, taste and experimentation. Here are some selection guidelines:

**Above** With knitwear, colour and yarn textures are tried out together to build up a storyboard.

**Below left** Here, rubber has been printed to look like Aran knitwear and Scottish tartan.

**Below right** Different prints are used to create a stylish and unexpected effect.

**Above** Fabric must be selected firstly by handle and then by its other inherent properties, such as warmth or shine, colour, decorative effect or how well it makes up.

**Opposite, left** A subtle use of the optical effect, vibrating colour in printed stripes.

**Opposite, right** Printed sheepskin combines the exotic with the cosy.

Crush the fabric a few times in your hand to feel the surface and assess its warmth, coolness, dryness, slipperiness, etc. What is the fabric's personality? What is the fibre content?

How does the fabric recover from your handling? Check the fabric between your thumbs for stretch and recovery. Gently pull in the grain and bias directions. Fold or drape the fabric to see how it hangs. Tease the threads to see if it will pull apart or fray easily.

Check the selvedges to see whether the fabric is straight. Off-grain fabrics will not hang properly, and in colour-wovens and plaids, hemlines and matching seams will be misaligned.

Look for weaving or dyeing irregularities. Hold a fabric up to the light if you think it is patchy. Colours can look very different in shop lighting compared to daylight; if you are trying to match a colour ask if you can take it to another light source.

Knit and woollen fabrics are prone to pilling. Rub the surface and see if fibres come off or roll into balls.

Printed fabrics should be checked for even printing and correct alignment. Hold up the print against the body and at arm's length to see what the scale of the design looks like.

Silk materials and cheap cottons sometimes have a starch called 'size' applied at the weaving or finishing stage. This washes out later and leaves the fabric limp. Rub the surface to see if a fine powder appears.

If there is information available about wash-care or finishes, take note. You cannot complain later if you mistreat a fabric.

(For a list of fashion and textile terms for fabric qualities, consult the glossary on page 184.)

# Range building

Whether you design a single garment or a whole collection you will need to combine a number of fabric types. This can be as simple as choosing supporting fabrics such as linings and **interlinings** or as complex as putting together a story of different weights and qualities to build up a range. In designing a collection it is necessary to work out a balance between the number of items you are going to make, the core fabrics and the accent or highlight fabrics that are appropriate. If you use too many fabrics and colours the collection will look uncoordinated; too few and it risks looking dull or repetitive. Some fabrics need to be simple and classic as foils to the eye-catching items.

Put your fabric cuttings together with your design illustrations or roughs. Always keep in mind the body type and lifestyle of the market that you are designing for. In the design room of a fashion company the concept and storyboarding processes are an extensive part of range building and are frequently reviewed. Fabrics that are too expensive or 'difficult' are eliminated. You will find that you have your own preferences and style for fabrics and trimmings; these choices will establish your image and unique identity, so care and consistency in building your signature choices is advisable. Many famous fashion designers have popularized particular fabrics: Coco Chanel was known for her use of easy-to-wear jersey and braid-bound tweedy woollen suits, while Issey Miyake is famed for his use of felts and pleated polyester.

The garment design and the fabric should not battle for attention but complement each other. The general principles of design – proportion, rhythm and an awareness of the human body in movement – need to be borne in mind and applied not to just one garment but to the whole 'look', when range building. If your collection is to be shown on a runway, rehearse, in your mind's eye, the order in which you would like to present the outfits for maximum impact. A model line-up helps you to balance the range, swap items around and make decisions about accessories and styling. In commercial ranges the collection is grouped in 'stories' of colour and fabrication to help the buyers to merchandise it in the shops. Coloured thumbnail sketches or photographs of your finished items, both separately and worn together as outfits, are useful as aids to range building and later to selling a collection.

# Fabric suppliers

Sources of fabric need to be reliable and competitive. Price, delivery times, export and import regulations, fluctuating currencies and consistency of quality are key issues. A good relationship with suppliers is the backbone of a successful design line. Manufacturers and fabric sources vary in their approachability and generosity to students. Happily, you will not be tied into producing multiples of your designs, so it is possible for you to buy fabrics in small quantities and from unusual sources and at retail. You may even have the opportunity to make or adapt your own fabrics if you have access to printing, knitting or weaving facilities.

## Textile mills

Textile mills weave or knit fabric that is sold directly to garment manufacturers or wholesalers or sold through agents. Mills tend to specialize in a specific process or type of fabric; for example cotton shirtings for daywear, luxury woollens for suits and separates and Jacquard woven silk for evening brocades. Fabric bought direct from the mill may often be less expensive than if it is handled by an agency, but the mill often demands a very large minimum quantity. A fashion designer can work directly with fabric designers and the mill to produce special or exclusive materials.

## Converters

Converters buy or commission unfinished (**greige**) goods from mills and have them printed up, dyed, waterproofed, etc by contractors according to their market forecasts. Converters work closely with manufacturers and designers.

## Importers

Labour costs, availability of raw materials and copyright mean that certain fabrics have to be imported. Often they have to be ordered in advance on indent or **quotas** to suit trade cycles and opportunities. Importers will warehouse these, and, while some are paid for at the time of order, some are sold from stock. Working with importers reduces the complexity of shipping documentation and import duties, currency fluctuations, holiday dates and language difficulties.

## Agents

Agents are the representatives of fabric manufacturers and do not carry any stock. They will help negotiate and organize the ordering and delivery of merchandise, either locally or through importers. The agent can be a wily salesperson, but he or she can also help you to get a better service from the supplier.

## Wholesalers

These suppliers buy finished goods from mills and converters and offer stock while it lasts. Sometimes the firms specialize in particular fabrics. Wholesalers do not always have a continuity of colours and textile types. Established fashion companies will be able to place orders and agree credit terms, but as a fashion student you will probably have to visit them and buy on a cash-and-carry basis.

## Jobbers

Basic fabrics can often be carried over into the next season, but sometimes orders are cancelled or too much material made. Mistakes, rejected dye lots and fashion fads have to be sold off quickly to turn around the investment. Manufacturers try to keep stock as low as possible as fabric deteriorates, goes out of season and costs money to store. Jobbers are specialists in buying up the excess at discount

Unusual materials call into play diverse sensory effects that can be used to make dramatic fashion statements. As in basket-weaving, this wicker dress was woven as a three-dimensional form. It gently undulates like an octopus in motion.

Fabric and fibre fairs are held biannually in different fashion cities around the world. Première Vision in Paris and Interstoff in Frankfurt are the largest and most prestigious. Spinners and weavers will commission fashion designers to make promotional ranges for their exhibition stands.

or acting as agents for manufacturers. They offer fabric to retail outlets, market stallholders and small companies for immediate delivery at low cost. This fabric, and the garments made from it, are known as **cabbage**.

**Retailers**

Fabric shops and department stores will have obtained their stock from most of the sources listed above. You will be able to buy small quantities of a wide range of qualities but at a price almost three times the wholesale cost with tax.

# Fabric fairs

The major fabric fairs are Interstoff, held in Frankfurt; Première Vision in Paris; IdeaComo in Como, the International Fashion Fabric Exhibition in New York and The Cloth Show in London. The top yarn shows are Pitti Immagine Flati, held in Florence, and Expofil, held in Paris. Unfortunately, a fashion student will not easily be able to gain access to these venues without an invitation or industry pass. Your college course may arrange visits for you, and some fairs occasionally allow students to take notes on the last day of trading.

# In the studio V

# The college studio

The layout of your college design studio may be arranged in a number of different ways. It might emulate a design studio or that of a small factory environment, depending on the course structure and the balance of students to technical assistants and staff. Some colleges allow you to have your own work station and pin board; others will take an open-plan approach and a first-come-first-served attitude to space. The early bird does well by this, but many colleges are open all hours and the atmosphere in the evening or at the weekend in an open-plan studio can be more stimulating than at eight o'clock on a Monday morning. Whatever your preference or your college policy, it is wise to be present at staffed times and to learn to share machine time, tutors and space equably.

## Basic equipment

Central to the fashion design studio is the pattern-cutting table. Tables are usually constructed for the average height of a woman, that is, 92 centimetres (36 inches) high, and approximately 120 centimetres (48 inches) wide to allow for the widths of fabrics. The length of the table needs to be at least long enough to cut a full-length dress pattern – about four metres (or yards) or longer. The table is used both for drafting patterns and also for cutting the sample in fabric. It has a very smooth surface to allow silky and delicate fabrics to roll over it without snagging.

The studio machinery is industry-standard in most instances, with some special equipment such as overlockers, seam coverers and binders and a steam-iron or pressing table. Sometimes you will have access to embroidery and knitting machines. The machinery provision will depend on what relationship your course has to technical practice versus design practice. All sewing and pressing machines are potentially hazardous, so you are required to have a safety induction and to use them under supervision.

**Below left** You may be given a creative space that you can decorate with your own pictures and work in progress.

**Below centre** The pattern-drafting table and the dress form are essential pieces of fashion-studio equipment.

**Below right** Learning how to make garments to a professional standard using industrial machinery helps you design commercially-viable clothes.

Not all colleges have a staff of technical assistants or machinists on hand for making up clothes. You may have to learn to do this yourself without aid; most colleges will also expect you to have a sewing machine at home. There will usually be pattern-drafting tutors on the permanent staff. They will teach the basics by demonstration in the studio and troubleshoot problems one-on-one by circulating among the students or through a system of informal appointments.

The dress stand (or tailor's dummy) is an essential piece of studio equipment for testing the viability of patterns. It is a solid torso, usually moulded in plastic and covered with thin padding and tightly fitted linen. It is adjustable in height and some have retractable shoulders to ease the slipping off of a close-fitting style. There are a wide variety of stands for men, women and children of different sizes and age ranges, and also for trousers, eveningwear, lingerie and maternity clothes. There are also detachable arms for jacket styles. Stands can be adapted by adding padding if designing for portly or unusual figures.

The exterior is usually divided into eight vertical panels providing a guide on which most garments can be fitted. However, you can change the seam guides by the use of narrow black tape. Attach these with lills (the smallest pins), which come out easily when you wish to move the tape markers. Taping helps you to see through the **toile** (or muslin in the US) to get the darts in the right place and to keep the grain line of the fabric in balance. Necklines and armhole positions can also be draped on in tape and pinned into position when correct. A stand is extremely useful as a surrogate body as it allows you to rotate the garment and evaluate your work from a distance. It is vital for draping and modelling techniques. However, it is fixed in a static posture and should not be relied upon for all solutions; many design flaws only come to light when worn by a real body.

# Measuring and mapping

In the past, skilled tailors came to observe that people could be divided roughly into body types and fitted by effectively following a few rules of ratio. In the nineteenth century the art of tailoring also became a science. The Victorians were inspired by the writings of Charles Darwin and the new art of documentary photography to catalogue and measure the variety of human form, at home and in distant lands. The science of anthropometry, the mapping of the body, was developed. Varying methods of measuring the body for tailoring were devised, employing templates, or **blocks**, which were based on the division of the body into symmetrical sections (for example, front torso to centre, top sleeve and undersleeve). Today, new technology, such as 3-D body scanners that capture accurate measurements, are improving data and providing the true sizing of different geodemographic groups.

### Standard sizes

As manufacturers organized themselves and their products, standardized sizing, pattern-drafting, grading and labelling procedures evolved. Although these methods of measuring still differ from country to country, it is now possible, thanks to the work of the British Standards Institution and the US Department of Commerce, to designate the sizes of garments internationally to help reduce confusion. The United States, where there is a wider range of sizing categories than in Europe, uses the imperial measure: that is, yards, feet and inches. In Europe and the Far

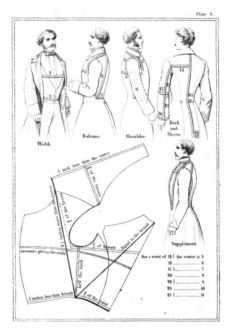

**Top** The art of the tailor lies partly in the ability to construct clothing that hides the imperfections of the body.

**Above** Standard measurements are frequently revised as changes in peoples' health and nutrition continue to affect the average body shape.

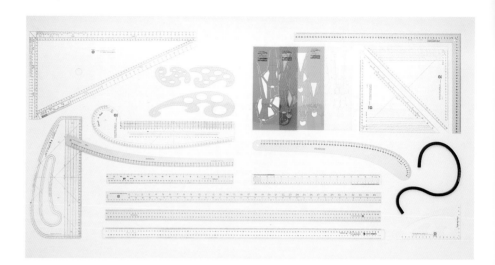

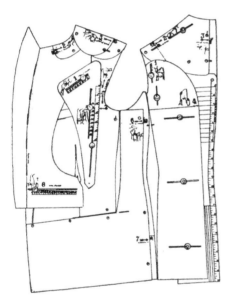

**Top, left and right** Pattern-drafting equipment.

**Above** This patented pattern maker could be adjusted in two minutes to a customer's measurements to draft a made-to-measure pattern.

**Overleaf** The detritus of the design studio.

East, garments are commonly sized in centimetres. Always enquire whether your manufacturer works in metric or imperial (see the size chart at the end of the book).

The average woman in the United Kingdom, the United States and Middle Europe is 163 centimetres (64 inches) tall (5 centimetres or 2 inches taller than she was fifty years ago), pear-shaped rather than hourglass and wears between a size 12 and 14 (US size 10 and 12). Most fashion companies produce women's garments between sizes 8 to 14 (or US 6 to 12), despite the fact that a third of all women are larger than a size 16 (US size 14). Menswear is more broadly defined. Manufacturers sell garments to buyers in a size range that will depend on the market for which they are aimed, with young or middle-aged fashion having different requirements and expectations of fit. Today more suppliers are beginning to offer clothing in 'plus' (outsize), petite and tall ranges, and classic trousers are often sold in a variety of leg lengths. Swimsuits and 'bodies' are also offered in different torso lengths. Hosiery is sold in a wide range of leg lengths.

In spite of two centuries of accurate measurement, however, people still claim to have trouble finding clothes to fit. A survey by Kurt Salmon market researchers found that in the United States, $28-billion worth of clothing is returned to the stores due to poor fit. Where the fit is critical, for example in sportswear, it is important to be aware of how the body grows and what sort of movement must be allowed for in certain styles. When a particular fashion such as the hipster skirt or trouser comes into vogue, it also places a demand on the lingerie supplier to cut the line of underwear and tights lower on the stomach, and a 'new' measurement is taken. Such measurements are called specifications, or specs, and are written up on design illustrations to prevent ambiguity in cutting and making.

While you are a fashion student you will probably make samples to a model size 10 or 12 (US size 8 or 10). However, it is as well to bear in mind that, when you leave college and design garments to be graded into different sizes, fashion details such as pockets and seam lines must continue to look right on a narrower or larger fit.

Even if you do not plan to be a master pattern-cutter, you will need to understand the importance of measuring and transferring these measures to a pattern in

order to make your sketch, design lines and structure work. It is essential for the designer to have a comprehensive grounding in basic pattern-making for the major garment types in order to design well.

# Pattern drafting

## Pattern-drafting tools

For pattern drafting you will need a number of tools, and these can be bought from specialist haberdashers (notions stores) and suppliers to the trade:

Hard pencils (2H–6H) for drafting

Pencil sharpener and eraser

Felt-tip pens, red and black for marking patterns

French curve (for drawing and measuring curves)

Graders set square or triangle (for finding the bias grain)

Transparent ruler (preferably with slots to measure buttonholes and pleats)

Metre rule or yardstick (preferably marked with both measuring systems)

Tape measure

Tracing wheel

Paper shears

Pattern notchers

Awl or spike

Hole puncher

Sticky (transparent) tape and masking tape

Pins

Black seam tape

Pattern drafting can seem a very dry, dull and mathematical subject at first until the magic of it starts to work under your fingers and you realize the infinite possibilities that can be achieved with a snip here and a curve there. Very minor adjustments can make a great deal of difference to the fall of a collar or the balance of a garment. Your design confidence will grow if you can turn your drawings quickly and effectively into the real thing. There are two main ways of developing a garment shape: flat pattern drafting and draping.

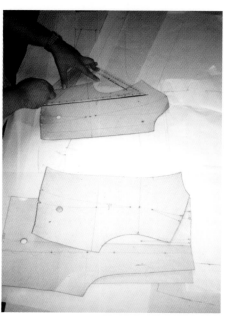

**Top** Sports clothing can be a fascinating and inventive field to design for as it is continually evolving. Here an ingenious hidden trouser lies under a skirt that preserves a lady's modesty while allowing her to sit side-saddle.

**Above** The designer drafts a new pattern by using a basic block as a foundation.

## Flat pattern drafting

Flat pattern drafting is precision drawing that requires accurate measurement and use of proportion, a neat hand and an ability to imagine the effect in three dimensions. Tailored garments have a logical structure of their own and often require stiffening fabrics and paddings. These and garments which outline or follow the contours of the body are most successfully developed from flat pattern drafting. Flat patterns are usually developed from a set of measured pattern blocks (see below). Flat patterns can also be drafted using computer software that is programmed to plot the entered measurements. Very close-fitting garments such as corsets and brassieres that squeeze or distort the flesh should be flat-drafted and then remodelled on a real body.

## Draping

Draping – also known as modelling on the stand – entails fitting a toile fabric – a lightweight cotton muslin – on a dressmaking mannequin of the appropriate size, or on a real body. When the shape and fit are correct, the toile (muslin) is removed and copied on to pattern paper or card. Draping techniques work best with jersey fabrics and generous amounts of soft materials. It is also used to work fabric 'on the bias', that is, across the grain, so that it moulds to the body shape and moves well.

## Blocks

College courses will differ as to how they approach the art of flat pattern making. The system of working two-dimensionally is fast, economically viable and indispensable to the fashion industry. Some courses prefer you to develop blocks – also known as slopers – from an individual set of measurements; others will issue you with standard-size blocks for bodice, jacket, trouser and skirt.

The block is a foundation pattern constructed to fit a specific figure. It is used as a basis for interpreting and making a pattern for a new design. It can be used again and again, so it is usually cut in heavy card or plastic to stand up to lots of handling. The style lines of the design developed from it may change dramatically, but the fit will conform to that of the basic block used. Usually the standard blocks are accompanied by the garment toile that they represent so you can see what the fit or 'ease' is like and adjust accordingly. Couture and bespoke-tailoring customers will have blocks drafted from their personal measurements, from which all their clothes can be made. Fashion samples are usually made up in the average model size 10 or 12 (US size 8 or 10), sometimes with 3.5 centimetres (about 1½ inches) added length in the back and leg for the additional height of a fashion model.

# Developing the pattern

You are likely to be expected to discuss your design ideas with various people at different stages during the development of your sketches. Sometimes technical staff will point out difficulties or restrictions that you may not have thought of, and you will have to go back to the drawing board.

When you have clarified the design, you will be shown how to draft a first paper pattern. The pattern-drafter copies the block by tracing around it and then superimposes the style lines of the new garment to be developed. It is important to transfer as many details as possible from the basic block to the new pattern, including the centre front (CF), centre back (CB) and the waist and hip lines. Sometimes the pattern will need various manipulations to be slashed and moved and redrawn, so it is necessary to be aware of how the grain is affected.

The diagrams in the middle below show how a basic bodice can have the bust dart position changed in many ways while still keeping the essential fit. The images on the left and right show how the style and seam lines and darts are used to pinch out or 'suppress' fabric to give the garment shape. The same process is used to shape the area between the waist and the hips in a skirt or pair of trousers.

'When we make the pattern, I advise them. I'll say, "Well, you could do it this way or maybe it's better to do it that way", and actually we work together as a team. So I have to get used to each student and help them in their own way – I don't want to influence too much.' Pattern-cutting tutor Jacob Hillel

# The toile

The pattern needs to be tested in calico or a fabric similar in weight and behaviour to the final garment material. The first fabric sample is called a toile (pronounced 'twahl'), from the French for a lightweight cotton fabric – in the US it is called a muslin. White or ecru material is easier to work with than dark or patterned cloth. Without the distractions of colour or design it is possible to see the cut and fit of the pattern more clearly. The centre front and back should be marked clearly with long, straight lines using pencil on wovens or felt-tip pen on knits. The waist and hip lines also need to be marked as reference points for fitting and altering.

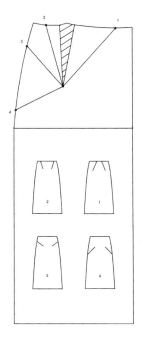

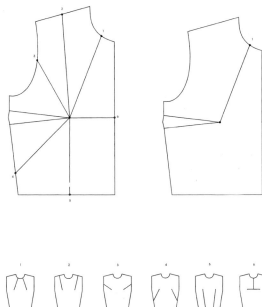

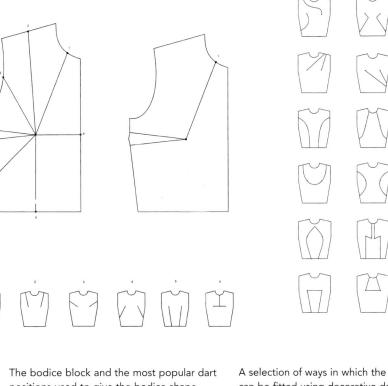

A simple skirt block and the different dart positions used to shape it to the waist.

The bodice block and the most popular dart positions used to give the bodice shape.

A selection of ways in which the front bodice can be fitted using decorative dart positions.

# Making the toile

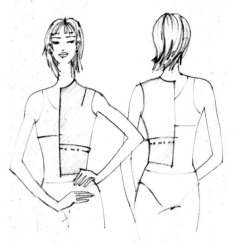

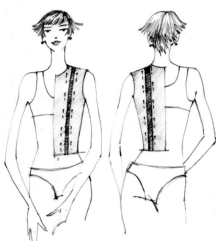

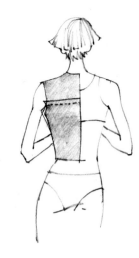

To alter the length of a bodice, pin out the excess, or tape in extra material under the ribcage.

Bust- and back-width adjustments can be made with a vertical addition or subtraction through the bust point to the waist or through the shoulder-blade line.

A flat back will need a horizontal adjustment and fabric taken out under the arm.

Add fabric for square shoulders or if you wish to use shoulder pads.

Square or sloping shoulders can affect the fit of the side seams.

Small darts are used to take excess fabric out of a neckline.

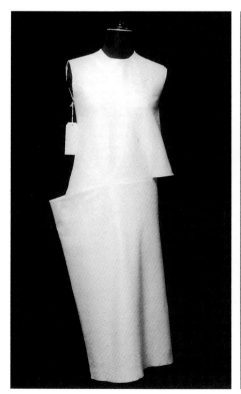

A tutor helps adjust the toile for a better fit.

A shawl collar edge-to-edge coat.

An asymmetric flared dress.

A tunic cut across at the hip to create a pocket.

A tunic with appliqué detail.

A crinoline and corset.

The toile is made up and fitted on a dress stand, mannequin or person. The seams are not overlocked or bound so that the garment can be opened and adjusted again speedily. Alterations are made and instructions can be written onto the toile in pen or tailor's chalk. Paper or fabric can be attached to the toile to restyle details such as lapels, and style lines can be redrawn and later transferred with a tracing wheel onto the paper pattern. Fabric moves and stretches, and the pattern may need to be adjusted to take account of the nature of the fabric used. This applies particularly to the patterns of jersey or draped styles, which often have to be made up several times to correct the fabric dropping and the inherent bias stretch of lighter-weight materials. In a symmetrical garment it is sometimes reasonable to make only half of the toile.

When you make a collection it is common practice to show your toiles, on models, to your tutors at a 'line-up'. This way the balance and proportion of the whole range or line can be seen, discussed and modified before you cut your fabric. For toile-making you will need fabric shears, small sharp embroidery scissors, a soft pencil, coloured pencils or fine felt pens, pins and a sewing needle, a seam ripper/ unpicker, sticky tape and masking tape, a sewing machine and threads.

# Markings and notches

When the pattern is deemed to be correct, it is marked up properly. Show all the grain lines; these are marked parallel to the centre front or centre back except in a few cases. Grain lines on sleeves and flared skirt panels are usually marked through the centre. If the pattern is to be used on a one-way print or fabric with a nap, such as velvet, mark the grain line with arrows to show the direction of the nap. The lengths of seams are aligned and checked. Seam allowances are added and marked with the allowance to be taken. Mark dart points, pocket positions and trimmings with an awl or hole punch. The two sides of a dart must always be identical in length. Sometimes buttonhole positions are drilled with a neat hole.

In order for the garment to hang straight, 'balance points' are notched in at 90 degrees to the edge to mark the grain at centre front and centre back, and seam-matching points are placed. Matching points are never put in the centre of a seam, but placed off-centre so that the next piece cannot be attached upside down by accident. This is especially important in styles such as slim panelled skirts. Single notches are used in the front; pattern pieces and double notches at the back. Multi-panelled styles add more notches for each successive panel as it goes round to four notches at the centre back. Notches are used to mark off the positions for darts, placing zips or in a position that would be helped by a little snip of the fabric to ease the seam on a curve (for example, at the waist or under the bust on a princess-line dress).

Mark the size of the pattern and number of pieces to be cut (for example, 'pocket bag x 4'). Make sure you give the pattern a name (or number), and put your name on it. Place all the pieces in a stack, and put one hole through all of them about 10 centimetres (4 inches) from the top edge. Either put a pattern pin through them and hang them on a rack, or fold them together neatly and put them in an envelope with your name and corresponding spec or illustration on the front.

**Above** Draping on the stand is about working with fabric and body together; it is difficult to master and is therefore a highly-regarded skill. The artistry lies in achieving a flattering shape with the least amount of cutting and contrivance.

**Opposite** A draped and knotted dress.

# Draping on the stand

Draping is sculpting with fabric and is most effective when using soft fabrics in fairly generous quantities. Fabric can be draped tight to the body and controlled with invisible stitching, or hung loosely in swags. Real models can be used to work the fabric on. However, because it can take a considerable time to get the effect right, it is preferable to use a dress stand for most of the work. Draping can be very frustrating, yet is hugely rewarding when it works. It is vital to work with the inherent weight and spring of the material. Fabric that is draped on the bias or cross-grain stretches and behaves differently to the same fabric draped on the straight grain. Experimenting with the direction of the grain can be fascinating.

It is useful to use a Polaroid or digital camera when draping as it is hard to remember all the permutations you have been through. When you have a pleasing effect, take a picture; then at the end of the day you can review the variations and return to the most successful. You will also have a record for your sketchbook that proves that you have been working.

When the design looks right and has been loosely stitched into place, try it on a real model. Then the fun begins. Drapes have a habit of falling out of place and spoiling everything as soon as the person moves. Alternatively they can do strange and wonderful things and set you off on a whole new path. When you think you have the style tamed, take the toile off the model or stand and smooth it out flat. Everything must be meticulously marked. You may need to piece extra fabric together if you are cutting on the bias and run out of material. Use broad sticky tape and felt-tip pens to indicate the direction of folds. Mark the centre front, shoulder line, seams and armholes and snip off any extra bits. Straighten up the grain line and smooth out sketched lines with a French curve or rulers. Then

## Guidelines for draping

Mark the straight grain and bias of the toile fabric in different-coloured felt-tip pens.

Pin the fabric in the centre front (or back) of the dress stand and establish your neck opening.

Pin the shoulder seam in place, checking for placement.

Pin the side pieces in place and clip the armhole area.

Pin or tape folds and pleats into place.

Stand back and observe the results. Use an instant camera to take pictures of your draping work in progress.

If necessary, make corrections, readjust gathers, move seam lines, darts, folds, etc, or add fabric where the garment requires it.

When the garment fits correctly, mark the neckline, armhole, waist position, centre front and centre back with a soft pencil or fine felt-tip pen.

Remove the fabric from the form and transfer all markings to paper. True up all straight edges and curves.

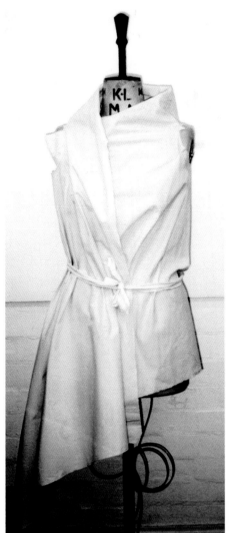

redraw or trace through with a tracing wheel to mark the pieces on pattern paper. Draped styles are often very odd shapes and you will need to mark in the top and bottom hemlines and probably lots of notches and arrows to show the directions in which to fold them. Try to sew it together as soon as possible. It is very easy to forget everything overnight.

The most useful tip in pattern-drafting is to be neat and methodical about marking up your final pattern, however messy the process of arriving at it has been. Fold it carefully and put it in a large envelope with an illustration on the front. Weeks later you will not want to come back to a crumpled piece of paper with bits of old tape stuck all over it.

Most pattern development is a mixture of flat pattern-cutting and draping. Even if you prefer to use blocks, you will find that the stand is very helpful for determining the roll of a collar and lapel or the flare and fall of a skirt. There is no right or wrong way to translate your drawings into fabric. Some styles are very difficult to get right and may take three or four patterns or toiles to be 'just so'.

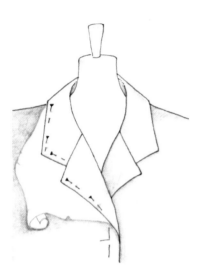

'It's not as easy as it looks. I start with the idea of a movement, and this season I wanted to have the nonchalance of something falling down. I like to change a movement, change the way something falls. It's like cutting an attitude into the clothes.' Designer Ann Demeulemeester

# Cutting the sample

When you are satisfied that the toile is correct and that you have made the alterations to the paper pattern, you can cut the sample out in the intended fabric. Plaids and print designs may require careful laying of the pattern pieces so that the final effect is pleasing. Some fabrics, such as corduroy, have a direction or nap that causes the material to shade. The pattern will have to be put down in a single direction. Stretch fabrics may stretch in one or more direction and this needs to be allowed for; cut them in their 'relaxed' state.

Roll or spread the fabric on the cutting table, and lay the pattern pieces flat on the fabric; they may be weighed down with heavy metal bars. There is no time for pins, which in any case may make the fabric wrinkle and cause inaccuracies. You should check the lay of the pattern to see how much fabric it takes and if the fit can be improved. While you have the pattern pieces drawn up on the cloth, make a sketch of the lay. If you have to make another sample, it will save time fitting the lay again. Sometimes the pattern, or even the design itself, needs to be revised to make a difference to the wastage if the fall-out is significant. Make sure that, where pairs of items are called for (sleeves, pockets, etc), two pieces of each are laid in.

The pattern pieces are outlined with a soft pencil or chalk, and the darts and pocket positions marked through holes in the pattern. Samples and toiles are hand-cut with shears, using the full length of the blades on straight edges and without lifting the fabric at all. Depending on the garment type, there may also be facings, fusible interfacings and trimmings to be incorporated into the finished garment. Cut these and match them up to the pieces with which they are to be fused. The

**Above** A design is very rarely perfect the first time it is cut. It often needs to be taken back to the pattern stage and altered.

**Below** This jacket uses a combination of cutting and draping techniques for its fit and flare.

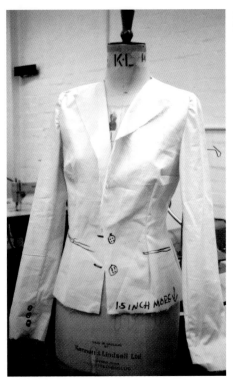

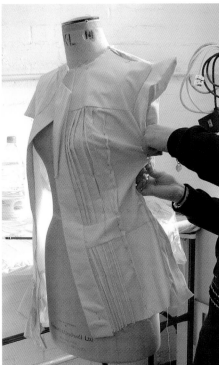

**Above** The stages of making a garment include marking the positions of seams and details, making changes and trying the piece on many times.

**Below right** Samples and toiles are hand-cut with shears, using the full length of the blade. Hold the pattern pieces down with the flat of your hand as you cut and always cut the notches as you come up to them.

fabric pieces are all rolled together and tied up with a strip of wastage, any zips or trimmings, and a sketch of the design, ready for assembly. This is called a bundle. Rolling is better than folding as creases are less likely to form. If you give the bundle to a sample machinist to make, discuss your design and any aspects that you need to work out.

# Sewing

A crucial aspect of your fashion training will be learning sewing skills. Some students will arrive at college having already made a number of garments on their own sewing machine and feeling fairly confident; others will never have threaded a needle. You may imagine that designing can be done at the drawing board, but it is in testing the design ideas by sewing a toile and discovering technical problems such as seam bulk or stretch that you learn how to design appropriately.

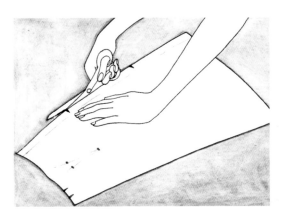

Industrial sewing machines are much faster, smoother and more specialized than their domestic equivalents, and require practice to use them effectively. Sewing takes patience and dexterity. Not everyone enjoys it, but the greatest motivation is seeing the garment that you have designed turn out well. Learning how to sew to a professional standard will also give you credibility with your future colleagues, help you to give specifications to a factory and comes in handy when you are struck by genius after hours or when something needs rectifying for a photographic shoot.

'I am amazed at how fast I can sew now. I didn't use to believe those stories about John Galliano running up dresses for people in the lunch break so that he could afford to go out clubbing. But I've run up a few things for myself now and it really makes you feel good when people ask you where you got it and you can say, "Well, actually…".' Second-year fashion student

Certain sewing techniques are associated with different levels of the manufacturing market. *Haute couture*, because of its use of expensive and delicate fabrics, merits expert sewing, more hand-finishing, bindings and linings. Lower down the market, handwork is rarely used, as it is costly and time-consuming.

Unusual materials such as plastics and leather may require you to use tissue paper or silicone spray; for others you may have to invent your own way of making them up. You may need to send garments to a specialist finishing house for pleating or elasticating, for example. Some machines can turn and apply bindings, flat-finish seams or apply elastics around neck and armholes. Twin-needle machines strengthen seams on jeans and workwear. Blind-stitch machines turn up hems with invisible stitches. Fashion knitwear students will learn how to put knitwear together with industrial linkers.

## Tailoring

Tailoring techniques include, and are an extension of, sewing. Tailoring is used most commonly in outerwear for men's and women's clothing. It is a method of combining and moulding fabrics together to create the desired shape on the body. It is in effect a combination of padding, tape stitching and pressing. Supporting fabrics and linings are added for strength and comfort. There is more handwork and attention to detail, making tailored garments more costly.

A tailor will baste (loosely tack together) a suit ready for the first fitting. When the adjustments have been made, it will be properly sewn together with a combination of machine- and hand-stitching. Wool fabrics respond very well to tailoring techniques as they have inherently pliable stretch and mould properties. However, tailoring is not restricted to the wool suit, and diverse fabrics from linens to brocades can be tailored.

# Fitting

Nuances of fit and finish can make or break a look. The enormous jeans market manages to update a single product year after year by concentrating on differences of fit. It is a good idea to test a toile not only on a dress stand but also on a real body in motion. The model can sit or stretch in the outfit and give a verdict as to comfort and wearability. Some people like a generous cut, others prefer to feel the garment close to the body.

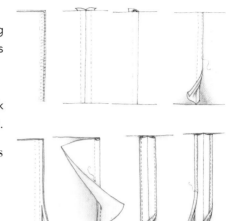

**Top, left to right** Straight overlocked seam, pressed open seam, top-stitched seam, flat-felled seam.

**Above, left to right** French seam, clean-finished seam, bias-binding.

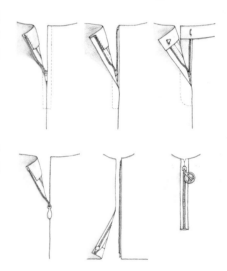

**Top, left to right** Centred zip, lapped zip, fly-front with zip guard.

**Above, left to right** Concealed (or invisible) zip, open-ended zip, exposed zip.

**Below, top to bottom**

The many linings and interlinings that go into a structured jacket have to be cut and trimmed away carefully in order to avoid bulky seams.

Much of the work in a tailored jacket is hidden on the inside; a jacket requires facings, interfacings, linings, shoulder-pads and seam bindings.

**Below right** Jetted pockets and pocket flaps are among the hardest elements to make well, as they must match in position and size. The buttonholes are often the last details to be finished on a tailored suit. If you do not have access to a professional buttonholing machine, be careful to use pins to avoid damaging the fabric.

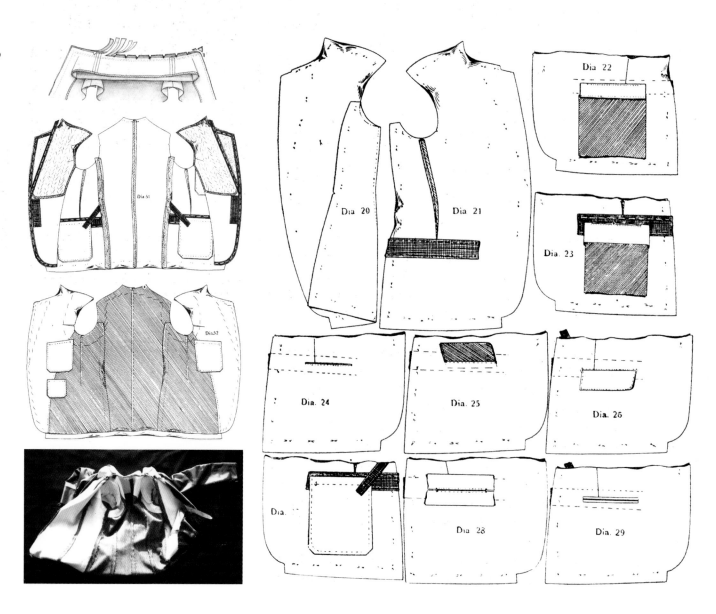

An active lifestyle dictates a certain ease of movement, and daywear is usually cut with this in mind. Fabrics have become very sophisticated, and many contain stretch polymers and materials with 'memory' so that shape is maintained in areas such as the knees and seat. Knit, jersey and Lycra fabrics are very forgiving. They do not need or look right with a lot of construction darts and seams.

This is the traditional sitting position for tailoring – despite appearances, it is very comfortable, the fabric can be spread across the lap and the knees can be used for easing and stretching the fabric into shape.

### Fitting tips

Some aspects of fitting need to be seen on a real body to ensure that the garment is not puckered or straining at the seams. When your model tries on the garment, notice if he or she is having trouble putting it on. Sometimes a longer zip or an extra button will solve the problem. If you are making a tight-fitting garment, there may be subtle adjustments around the shoulders, breast and seat to be made that cannot be discerned on the dress stand. Get your model to walk about in the outfit and see if he or she can sit down comfortably. Strappy and strapless evening dresses need to be checked for décolletage and slippage, preferably on more than one model. Draped styles need to be seen in movement and might need some stay-stitching into place. In fact, many skirts come into their own when walked and danced in.

Any style that is avant-garde or unpredictable certainly needs to be fitted to see what surprises may be lurking or need to be explained away. But classics, too,

**Opposite** A tailor makes a fitting of the first 'baste' of a bespoke suit.

**Left** A finished suit hits the catwalk.

**Above** Some styles should be tried on the body to check for fit and stretch.

need checking on a body because there is such a clear benchmark as to how these styles should hang and fit. There are many technical books showing you how to correct wrinkles and sags, and if you can't gently steam them out, you will have to do some unpicking or go back to the drawing board.

# Finishing

### Ironing and pressing

Learn to iron and press clothes properly. Many seams, facings and darts need to be properly pressed and finished as the garment is put together. This is called underpressing. Bound buttonholes and jetted pockets need to be flat-pressed to give a crisp, straight edge. Collar-points, cuffs, mitred corners, patch-pockets and waistbands need pressing with a point to turn them out neatly. Some facilities will

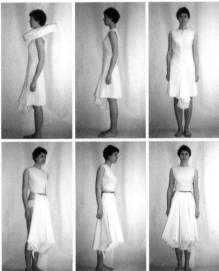

**Above and right** The development of the pattern and toile for a pleated skirt.

**Opposite** Keep a photographic record of all your work.

have industrial equipment and specialist items such as sleeveboards and hams for a rounded finish in tailoring. If you do not have access to these you can still get a good professional appearance with a heavy domestic iron that gives a shot of steam. Tailored garments and easy-to-crease items such as linen and cotton will not looked finished until they have been given a thorough pressing. Steam can be used to ease fullness into woollen fabrics.

Knowing the fabric content and care requirements of your materials is a good guide (see appendix for fabric types and the international care code). Always let the iron heat up to the correct temperature setting for the material. Test the iron out on a piece of scrap first, clean the sole plate of any sticky deposits and check that it does not leave calcium or rusty stains on the fabric when steaming. It is safest to iron through a lint-free muslin cloth, transparent enough to see what you are doing and slightly dampened for heavier fabrics. You can keep the cloth moist by spraying it with a spritzer bottle. Nylons and some synthetic mixes have low melt thresholds and surface treatments for fabrics can cause a material to scorch easily – iron the seams and hems of these on the wrong side to minimize shine. You might need to spray starch, silicone or waterproofing onto some fabrics to finish them. It is not a good idea to iron in knife creases on shirts and knitwear. Casual and sports clothing should look natural. Be careful with trouser creases; check on the body where you want them to fall because it is very difficult to undo them once pressed. When the clothes are still warm hang them up immediately to let them cool, don't pile up warm ironing as it will put in creases that you don't want. Some items, suits for example, can be 'refreshed' by steaming lightly over them while they are on the dress stand.

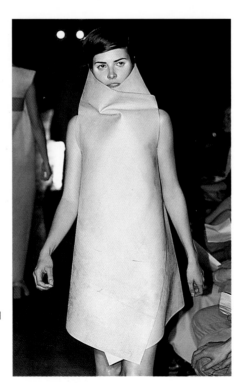

**Right** Simple and flat-pattern pieces slotted together and wrapped around the body form the basis of this collection that was developed on a wooden doll.

**Opposite** This 'origami' dress is a truly complicated piece of pattern engineering.

You may design innovative clothing using unusual materials such as rubber or plastic or employ techniques such as glueing and welding. Check which solvents these should be cleaned with and label your garments accordingly. Before a show or exhibition you will need to label your designs with your name, size and care labels. These usually go in the centre back at the collar and the waist. You will probably be asked to number the outfits in order of appearance and provide a photograph or instructions for wearing and accessories on the bag. Some garments cannot be folded or hung, delicate garments may need to be wrapped in paper tissue and it is often necessary to be as inventive with their care, storage and transportation as it is with the design.

**Below** Once you have mastered the basics of pattern-cutting and sewing, you will be ready to mix unusual combinations of cut and material. Here, shattered mirror pieces are being attached to a crinoline-like frame.

**Right** The finished dress, inspired by sparkling diamonds and worn to celebrate the millennium eclipse.

# The brief VI

**Top** An inflatable dress design for Barbie, the result of a second year project sponsored by Mattel.

**Above** 'Doing Smirnoff was a laugh. I was out to enjoy myself. I really thought I never had a chance of winning it. I've never won anything in my life, so getting the award was one of the biggest honours, especially in front of such a famous cast of judges.' Nick Darrieulat, winning student.

# What is a brief?

The most popular and successful means of teaching fashion is by means of the project. A project is a sustained piece of work, usually lasting two to six weeks and incorporating both research and practical skills. The title, tasks, aims and objectives of the project are set out in a brief. You will probably be asked to carry out your first brief during the vacation before you start your course. This first assignment is an introduction to the process of designing and later, during the assessment critique, or **crit**, to the presentation of work in front of staff and fellow students. The scope of a brief varies according to which specialism you are studying and also which stage of the course you have reached. The teaching staff will hold a briefing to present the project and discuss what is required of you. The brief will set out the task, tell you who will teach and mark the project, give the criteria for assessment, what work is to be submitted and when and how the crit will take place.

The purpose of a project brief is to develop your creativity to respond to a particular set of requirements. It is often a simulation of what may be required of the fashion designer within different market sectors. The brief gives you a chance to practise skills that will be required of you when you leave college and enter work. There will, however, be some significant differences.

# Types of brief

### The individual brief

The individual project brief can be set either by permanent staff or by visiting lecturers. It may be a problem that all those in your year group are set, or a task you are given personally in order to improve particular skills. You will be expected to respond to the requirements of the brief in your own individual way. Your response will be assessed and any marks given will be an indication of the progress that you are making.

### The sponsored brief

The sponsored project brief is set by a company – usually (but not always) a fabric or fashion company. The company will discuss the requirements with the teaching staff, and the results will be judged by a mixture of staff and company members, with marks and prizes awarded accordingly. Sometimes marks given by the college staff do not accord with the choice made by the sponsors because they are looking for different outcomes from the project – academic versus commercial considerations.

### The competition brief

The competition project brief is set by a company or external organization. Fashion competitions are a popular promotional ploy and are usually offered to colleges nationally. Prizes can include travel bursaries and placement awards. The results will be judged by the company team, and, unless you are a winner, you will be unlikely to know how your work has been appraised. Submitted work is not always returned so it is vital to make photocopies for your portfolio.

### The team brief

A team project brief requires you to interact with a group of students, some of whom you may not even know. Team projects are large in scope and frequently require you to consider marketing, labelling and costing issues as well as designing. Your own role may be defined by the group, and you will be expected to have brainstorming discussions and to cooperate with others within a simulated work environment. The pressure is intense, and sometimes you will be asked to mark your own or others' contribution to the team. Team project briefs are sometimes set by associated college departments or, more frequently, by companies and sponsors in collaboration with the college.

# What the brief asks of you

The brief aims to inspire you but also asks you to consider various conditions and constraints, some of which are related to the real-life conditions within the fashion market and others which are to do with academic requirements. You will probably not enjoy all of the projects. The brief will usually tell you what the overall aims of the project are and what objectives you should be able to demonstrate by the end of the project to enable you to measure your own progress.

# Aims and objectives

The emphasis on different aims and objectives will vary with the brief, but broadly speaking, the common criteria for assessment are that you should learn and be able to demonstrate:

The ability to research and apply research in a creative, independent and appropriate manner

The ability to analyse and resolve design and communication of design problems

Creative and intellectual inquiry and risk-taking in design solutions

Skill, imagination and originality in exploring techniques, materials, imagery and colour

The ability to synthesize your own ideas within your chosen fashion pathway

A grasp and understanding of industrial/professional roles and methodologies

The ability to work as an individual or as a team member

Good working practices and presentation skills in visual, oral and written form

Time-management, self-direction and self-evaluation

The fulfilment of your creative and intellectual potential and resolution of your own interests and design aspirations within the parameters of the brief and course curriculum

The brief will ask you to solve a specific task or choice of tasks. Sometimes this will be very clearly stated. At other times the brief may be fairly difficult to understand; a significant part of the exercise is to interpret the puzzle. The project brief will state the conditions or parameters that you must observe. Some probable examples are described below.

## Occasion and season

It is necessary to have an idea of the occasion for which you are designing, and this can be defined by the situation, time of day or season. The brief will often state the required season or event. A fashion student is expected to see around the next corner; fashion designers must create and confirm the trends rather than follow them.

**Top** Winning outfit for an Adidas-sponsored sportswear competition.

**Above** 'What's been good about this project is that you get do a bit of everything. Not one outfit is any one person's, we were all involved, and we really got to know one another. We're practically a family now.' Josh Castro, second-year student.

**Above** Shops that specialize in fabric trimmings, braids and buttons provide the details that can make all the difference to the success of an outfit.

**Above right** Street markets in some cities can be a good source for beautiful and inexpensive ethnic fabrics. Expect to buy a whole sari or batik piece rather than a cut length.

**Opposite, left** Traditional and unique fabrics such as cashmere and pashmina shawls, folk embroideries and French Jacquards can be a rich inspiration for fashion printers and weavers.

**Opposite, right** As a student you can take advantage of using special materials, such as brocades and laces, which are unavailable in large quantities, to make unique items.

'When I used to read about Yves Saint Laurent I thought, "What's he got to be so neurotic about?" But now I understand. Every six months you go through hoops of fire.' Designer Paul Frith

## Muse or customer

A brief sometimes asks you to imagine that you are designing for a specific type of consumer – of a certain size, age and gender – an individual who is a physical ideal or a source of inspiration. This can be a friend, model, film star and so on. You may be expected to build up a customer profile, including such elements as background, work, home, lifestyle and spending power. The point is to choose someone who you can imagine wearing your designs with the maximum impact.

## Target market

Becoming aware of the different market sectors is an important part of design education. You will frequently be asked to make market analyses and to place your designs within context. Designers vary widely in their interest in designing for different target markets. For some it is a pleasure and a creative challenge to design well to middle-market **price points**. Others enjoy the subtle shifts that take place within the classic clothing field, building up signature styling and customer loyalty over many seasons. For a few the interest lies in a niche market such as sportswear, lingerie or eveningwear. Project briefs are frequently set in collaboration with stores or designers who can give first-hand feedback as to the suitability of your designs for their market and customers.

## Choice of material and fabric

This element is often set out in the title of the brief. It is the 'problem' that you are asked to solve. Sometimes you are given a choice of themes to investigate, a list of contemporary exhibitions to see or a particular fabric to inspire you. Effectively you are restricted in some way in order to narrow the focus of your thinking and foster your creative ingenuity. The most common restriction is within a genre of

clothing or the choice of materials and fabrics to be used. For example, you might be set a 'shirt project' or 'the little black dress'. The first requires you to learn the technical skills of sewing regular shirt features such as plackets and collars but in an unrestricted styling and fabric choice. The second is to design an outfit that must work in one colour for a specific occasion.

Alternatively the choice may be open. Most fashion departments have an archive of materials to acquaint you with the qualities of fabrics, and you will be expected to experiment and work with new materials and techniques. You are also encouraged to make your own fabrics through knitting, printing or manipulating the surface of materials.

## Costing

The price of a fashion item in the shops will usually be determined by fabric price and making price, plus the profit margins that the retailer applies. In costing a garment, a few centimetres in the width of the fabric can make an enormous difference to the overall outcome, and patterns may need to be adjusted. Trimmings can increase the cost dramatically, quadrupling it by the time the garment is sold at retail and pricing it out of the market. While these financial considerations are not a major part of the design process in the fashion school, they are usually taken into account. You should be able to work out how much the item would cost to produce and thereby gauge whether it fits the marketing requirements of the project brief. You may be asked to produce costing sheets and **flats** and **specs** to clarify production issues.

In the designer sector the mark-up is usually in the region of 120 per cent. (The retailer will add a minimum mark-up of 160 per cent on this.) Calculate the probable retail price so that you can estimate whether the garment seems to look right for the price. In pricing a collection there is always the need to fix on an amount that strikes a balance between the value of the garment and what the customer will be prepared to pay for it.

**Opposite** John Galliano's final year collection was inspired by costume research into the 'macaronis' and 'incroyables' of the years after the French Revolution and led to the 'New Romantic' look that swept London in 1984.

**Overleaf** Some popular themes (such as the idea of uniforms and patriotism) are interpreted by designers in many different ways.

**Above** A streetwise outfit made valuable with collectible stickers and badges.

**Above right** These hand-embroidered tunics are inspired by old cross-stitch kits.

**Right** Recycling second-hand clothing, unravelling and knitting new sweaters from old and customizing are all popular ways for the fashion student to make ends meet. Here, cheap paper painting overalls have been customized for a 'trashy' look.

**Far right** By browsing in antique textile and costume shops you can discover the fascinating techniques used for making clothes in different eras.

Necessity is the mother of invention. Project briefs rarely require students to part with much money, and inspiration with budget fabrics is more highly rewarded than dull design using expensive fabrics. Recycling, charity-shop and market-stall buys and clever changes of use are all devices that students use to great effect. On the other hand, if you plan to work in couture and high-end fashion, it is helpful if you become used to handling luxurious materials without fear. It may be possible to find sponsorship for your fabrics from manufacturers, who have an interest in getting their wares in front of the public.

**Practical tasks**

The project brief will usually state how many items are to be made and some of the processes expected of you. The practical part of the work may be aided by the technical staff. Professional designers very rarely simply draw their ideas, however. Learning how to cut patterns and sew gives you an insight into the way that these practicalities impact on your designs (see Chapter V, 'In the studio'). Also important, from a practical viewpoint, is effective communication – both visual and verbal – so that alterations and mistakes are minimized. Time-management is another crucial skill. Bear in mind that there will be other demands on staff and technical sewing time, and that overambitious or unfinished work loses you credibility and marks.

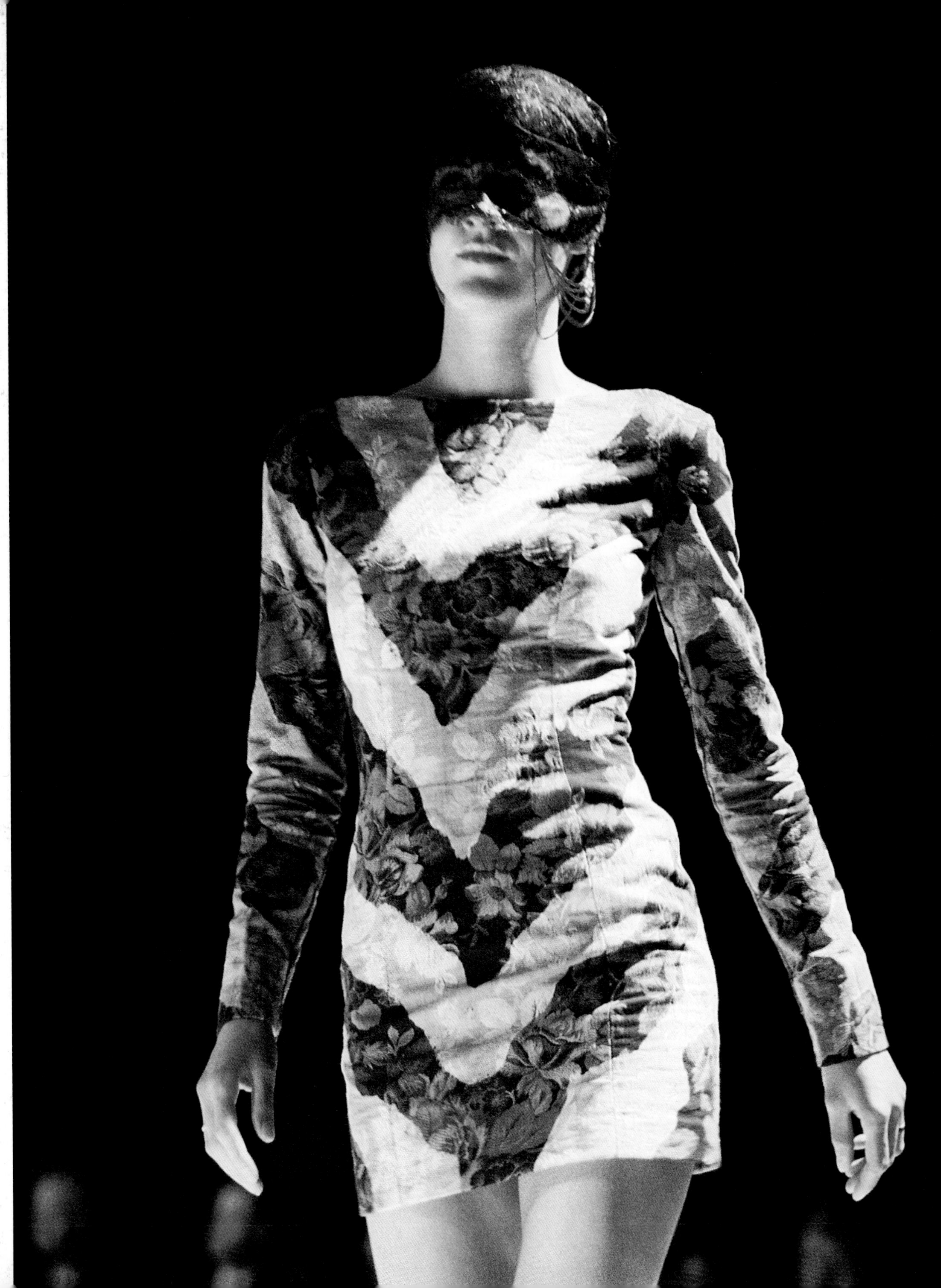

**Above**  Researching a project brief may involve background reading, as well as historical and practical research for fabrics and trimmings.

**Above right**  The concept for this outfit began with a reading of Patrick Süskind's novel *Perfume*. The model is wearing a cabinet jacket with perfume bottles on the shelves; the fan on her head wafts the scent into the audience.

# Inspiration

Fashion expresses the *Zeitgeist*, or spirit of the times, and therefore mirrors changes in society. In their search for inspiration, designers must learn to keep their eyes and ears open: to visit shows, shops, clubs, cafés, galleries and films; to read magazines, newspapers and novels; to party and to listen to music; and, above all, to people-watch and absorb the subtle and incremental aesthetic changes that take place in society. The key to creating new ideas is to jot down and mix the influences together in a sketchbook, then to blend this inspiration with your growing knowledge of fabrics, fashion details and target markets. With this constant fine-tuning of signals, you are in a better position to answer the brief and bring to it your own individual and intensely contemporary viewpoint.

'A good designer mirrors the times … I never party, but I watch people and I read – about how people's lives are being dominated by technology, for example – and I'll respond to that.'  Designer Joe Casely-Hayford

Colleges encourage students to paint and draw from life and nature as primary sources of design. Through close observation you gain a real appreciation of what you personally find inspiring, disturbing or beautiful in your environment. Popular visual research subjects include flowers, animals, landscape and urban themes such as architecture, city decay, bright lights and reflections. Sometimes a still life or model and environment will be set up in the studio as a focus for abstracting colour and line studies.

This eclectic look was inspired by the cheerful mixture of thrift shop sweaters worn with indigenous clothing that the student saw on a work placement trip to Africa.

# Personal creativity and style

A fashion-design student learns how to create new fashion by first understanding classic garments and their detailing. To become a fashion designer, however, you must do more than merely master a body of knowledge. You must look beyond that which already exists and find new combinations of ideas and materials which can satisfy people's needs and desires. Innovation comes with having the vision and courage to change the rules playfully.

When you first start to design, your tastes, like your personality, will have been partially formed by your background, social standing and experiences. This will be the core of your unique expressive spirit. What the staff will be looking for in your response to the brief is your own honest style, not a copy of your favourite designer's. This will evolve gradually, formed over the years by a passionate immersion in your work and by a keen appreciation of the work of your fellow students and professional designers.

While originality is prized, there is a balance to be struck; fashion does not find its mark if it is too far ahead of its time or outrages to the point of disregard. In creative surroundings you will find that you can discuss, show and achieve your ideas and be supported and stimulated by others.

> 'People do their own thing. Some do romantic things, some do conceptual, some do commercial. You can't compare us because we are doing what we want. If you are too competitive, you can drive yourself crazy because there are such a lot of good students here.' Second-year student

## Tapping creativity

There are many techniques for tapping into your creative spirit. Some of them can be taught, and some have to be experienced personally. Psychologists have identified two kinds of thinking that are useful for problem-solving: convergent and divergent thinking. Convergent thinking focuses the mind on aspects of the task that are already known and reduces the problem to one that you can manage, through skill, assembly and organization. Sometimes creative problem-solving depends on using the right tools, tricks, procedures or methods of analysis.

Divergent thinking requires a softer focus, dipping into the unconscious at will and utilizing the imagery to transmit ideas. It is not the same as daydreaming, more an ability to keep an open and aware mind. Have the courage to venture into the unknown, even if you don't understand where you're going or why these new paths will lead you to your solution. Try out ideas that look unlikely to work as well as the more defined ones. Many fashion designers spend time just handling and getting to know fabrics in a similar and meditative way. Later the solution as to how to use or place a fabric may suddenly spring to mind.

It can be creatively useful to 'put yourself in someone else's shoes'. A project brief may require you to design in the style of a known designer or a specified period or cutting method. This frame of reference allows you to try out already successful techniques and combinations of cut and detail and can give you insights

**Right** Florals are always in fashion, sometimes small and discreet, sometimes large and dramatic. Here they are 'storyboarded' for cosy knitwear designs.

**Opposite** Used here in this halter-neck dress, the rose motif looks fresh and summery.

**Above** Humour has its place in fashion. This tailored collection was inspired by ventriloquists' dummies.

**Opposite** Hussein Chalayan took a considerable risk with his final year collection in 1993. He made the clothes using paper, metal and magnets and then buried them in earth for six months to rot and rust. Electromagnets were used underneath the runway to make the fabrics vibrate and pull unexpectedly.

into the talents and tastes of others and the confidence to push your creativity further. Try to balance the approach with your own input.

Avoid an emotional or ego fixation on your own style; you are learning and need to be flexible. There will be design themes and qualities or intellectual ideas that particularly intrigue you and become the basis of your creative strengths and identifiable as your 'signature'. Your illustration and presentation techniques should also mature and develop into a personal 'handwriting' to complement the type of clothing that you are designing.

'Good taste' in fashion is a very mobile concept. It is time- and context-sensitive, partially instinctive and partially learned through some ground rules. It is often sensed intuitively rather than logically analysed. You may wish deliberately to flout good taste to shock or amuse. Alexander McQueen is an example of a renowned fashion designer who has consistently challenged ideas of taste and yet been fashionably of his time. Remember, the cutting edge moves extremely fast.

'When McQueen was at college they were trashing Galliano. When I was at college they were trashing McQueen. And then I went back last year and they were trashing me.' Designer Andrew Groves

### Stay positive

Criticism and judgement are important to progress and are the means by which you will improve on your performance. Do not confuse a critique of your work with personal abuse. Keep your ego under control. Designs cannot be imposed on people; they must be accepted by them. The ability to bounce back from disappointments is as much a part of the creative armoury as drawing and making.

And don't work too hard. Pace yourself – you need energy to be creative. Prolonged, intense focus and lack of sleep or nutrition is counter-productive and can stall the creative flow. It can be very upsetting if you find that you are at a standstill or unable to make decisions when all around you others are busy working. Sometimes you need patience, help, a break or a breakthrough in inspiration to set the wheels in motion again.

# Presentation
### Sketchbooks

Sketchbooks and visual notebooks are an essential part of the fashion student's kit. Used regularly and in conjunction with a camera, they form a portable and personal resource file of all that you find inspiring and stimulating. Your sketchbooks should record your evolving interests: impressions of artefacts, people and body poses, clothing and detail notes, colour and aspects of the environment. They can build over the years into a vast archive and supply of ideas that you can dip into.

It is worthwhile to keep a variety of sketchbooks on the go at any one time. Vary these in size and paper quality for convenience. A small book can be kept with you for thumbnail sketches and entering scraps of fabric and interesting design details seen while in shops or on public transport. Larger sketchbooks can be used to draw or paint from life or to work out more complex ideas. Sometimes the use of a larger scale gives weight to an idea. Layout pad is useful because of

the almost transparent quality of the paper, allowing body stances and silhouettes to be traced over quickly and details changed.

A good sketchbook will give those who see it a window onto your thinking processes and clues as to the origination of your design ideas. Your tutors will expect to look at your sketchbooks occasionally. They may also be assessed at the end of projects or at certain points in the academic programme. At times you may be asked to produce books with a more defined purpose: for example, a visual diary when on visits abroad or a source book that follows one line of discovery or theme. Knit- and print-design students will be expected to keep notebooks of colour and dye experiments.

### Tear sheets

Tear sheets (or swipes) are pictures torn out of magazines and newspapers, exhibition programmes, postcards, flyers and so on. Collect images that you like in order to help define a mood or look that engages you – but not to copy directly

**Left** A mood board on the theme of patchwork conveys the student's interest in cheap-and-cheerful effects and busy colour.

from. Tear sheets need not necessarily be contemporary. Second-hand bookshops, for example, are a rich source of unusual visual and reference material. Photocopies are useful, but beware of using too many or your work will take on a very 'secondary source' look.

## Mood boards

Once you have collected sufficient images and ideas from your research, it is possible to start the design development. You might be asked to do a 'mood board'. This is a more formal statement of your concept and intentions through pictures and scraps that you have carefully arranged and collated as if for a magazine page. Items are often pinned onto polyboard (foam core) rather than stuck down permanently. Polyboard is light and portable but can stand the weight of fabrics and trimmings and form a flexible focus for discussion of your ideas with your tutors.

**Above** Ideas for designs are first put down quickly as sketches or 'roughs'. Here a teddy-bear pattern is investigated.

**Right and opposite** An idea is tried out in a drawing, then made in miniature and finally made up full-size.

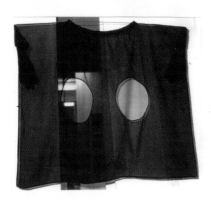

### Design sketches

During the early stages of answering a brief you need to sketch a number of ideas quickly in your sketchbook or on a layout pad. These are referred to as **roughs** and design developments. Mark or select the roughs you are happiest with and those that have elements you wish to explore further. Develop these and make a further selection. You can group designs according to various criteria such as the use of fabrics, silhouette, detail and so on. Design tutors will discuss these choices with you and help you to clarify and justify your decision-making.

### Storyboards

The brief will usually require you to make a presentation of your ideas through artwork as well as a prototype or garment. Storyboards are a series of finished presentation sheets or polyboards, which represent the whole 'story' of your solution to the brief. They will usually include a mood board, final illustrations and coordinated fabrics and trimmings, with a small amount of text to explain the theme, colours and market. Fashion courses have different approaches to this sort of presentation and may give students quite a lot of freedom when it comes to putting together artwork for a crit. This work often forms the core of the portfolio.

Your verbal presentation of your own design
process and your paperwork to staff and
fellow students at the crit is as important
as the outfit itself.

# The crit

The crit (or critique) is the occasion on which staff evaluate your response to the brief. It is both an objective and a subjective assessment of how you have fulfilled the requirements. It is also an exchange of ideas. The crit can be managed in a number of different ways, according to the type of brief. Sometimes it is a private assessment with a panel of teaching staff. At others it is a mini fashion show to which you will bring your dressed model. On these occasions the crit can be attended by the entire student group or a selection of students and staff, technical staff or invited visiting tutors. The panel will be looking for a solution that has not only answered the problem set by the brief but which also has balance, harmony, originality and a good choice of fabric and trimmings. Additionally, they will want to see that you have developed your design and practical skills.

Now and again only selected designs will be discussed in full in order to speed up what can be a very protracted process. The main points of success and failure that have come out of the project will be discussed and clarified. You will be given marks on the presentation of your work, both in its practical form and in the way that you explain and support your answer to the brief.

> 'During a crit students need to listen hard and learn to extract the useful information and facts from personal opinion ... A crit situation has all the dynamics of group therapy; it's usually very positive but often there are also confessions and tears. We all learn from it.'
> Second-year fashion tutor Sally Calendar

Most students and staff find that the crit is an enjoyable finale to a project. It is very satisfying to see your design finished and being worn, and also to see how others have tackled the same themes and yet come to very different conclusions. There will often be conflicting or varied points of view as to how successfully you have arrived at and achieved your objectives. If you are well-prepared and have rehearsed your presentation, this should not be a worry. The purpose of the crit is to help you appreciate your progress and resolve potential problems in your future work.

> 'If you know what you want to do because you have thought it through, it should have an inner logic and conceptual rightness – where all elements fit, dictate form and colour. Then you are away and it is straightforward production. Sweating over it for days can spoil it.' Final-year student

# Assessment

The grading scheme used for all marked projects will vary among colleges and courses. Some courses will award credits – marks or grades which you accumulate to allow you to progress to another or more advanced module (teaching unit) of the course. You can chart your progress by keeping a note of these marks and defining the strengths and weaknesses of your portfolio.

There is usually also a formal assessment of your progress at critical junctures of your course. You may be asked to put up a display of your work or show a portfolio to the staff team. Assessment is a matter of judgement, not simply of computation. At the final stage of a degree course you are marked by a panel of tutors, most of whom have been familiar with your work over an extended period. In most colleges the panel consists of at least one external examiner, who has been invited from industry or academia to ensure that there is a fair assessment of all students and that the required standards are observed.

The marks awarded at degree level are given a classification: first-class honours, upper second, second and third class. Some colleges award a pass or a pass without honours and fail. (Other qualifications such as certificates and diplomas award distinction, merit and pass classifications.) Usually there are marks for written work, such as a thesis or business report computed into the total; the balance and percentage given to contextual studies will vary in different establishments. In the unlikely event that you fail your degree, your college is required to indicate to you what the problems were and they may suggest a resit. If you are unhappy with your marks at any point during your education, you should make arrangements to see your tutors and discuss the problem. Staff are keen to see their students do well, and all colleges have appeals systems and some social-welfare programmes in place to help those in difficulties.

# The final collection – and beyond VII

# The final collection

Your last project brief, often called the 'final collection', should build on the individual successes that you have achieved over your years at college. This is the range that will launch you into the professional world. Essentially it is you who write your brief for your final collection. You may be expected to write a rationale, or explanation, of your intentions to help you to resolve your ideas. This will be presented together with your drawings, fabric selections and any other relevant data to the teaching staff and possibly also to external examiners or others invited to discuss your presentation and help you make your final garment selection. It can also function as a 'press release' to send out to the media, potential employers or buyers.

By this stage of your fashion course you will have identified the market and the type of person for whom you would like to design. Over the years you will have established a design identity. You will have an appreciation of the complex and competitive industry into which you are stepping, and the supporting work, photographs and illustrations in your portfolio will indicate that you are ready for your first professional brief. Fabrics, colours and your decisions about silhouette and design details will all be handled with a confidence that has grown and blossomed. You will have gained a variety of skills and technical knowledge to produce clothing appropriate to your specialism.

Your final-collection designs should look strong and include both important directional ideas and less dramatic pieces. When your designs have been approved in the presentation crit, you are ready to go to the pattern-making stage. There will probably need to be a number of adjustments and changes to your plan before the collection takes form and the toiles (muslins) meet with approval at the **line-up**, or review, of your collection before the styles are made up. For some, the practical making of their collection is the most enjoyable aspect of all.

> 'A collection can end up looking quite different from what you had in mind. It is quite hard to control; it has a life of its own; it jumps out of your hands. You look at it on the day of the show, when everything is put together, and it has changed. You think: "How did that happen?"'
> Designer Suzanne Clements

# The college fashion show

The fashion show of an established designer differs markedly from that of a student collection. The professional show gives retail buyers and the press a first view of a new commercially available collection. It is also a public-relations exercise that fuels the supply of pictures and stories to magazines, and, increasingly, it is an entertainment in its own right. The chief members of the college fashion-show audience, by contrast, will be staff, along with students, parents and a sprinkling of sponsors and manufacturers on the lookout for fresh employees and ideas. Some colleges feel that it is educationally decisive for fashion students to have the simulated experience of the catwalk show since many will meet with it later in their careers. The critical pacing of your workload and the ability to focus and present a cohesive range that is both creatively exciting and relevant to your future aspirations are assessable outcomes of the final-collection brief.

**Below**  Each student supplies shoes and accessories for their outfits.

**Bottom**  Students help with the make-up before the show.

**Below right**  Checking the line-up for fit and details backstage.

**Opposite**  Rehearsing the models for walk and timing before the show.

You will have worked very hard on your final collection and will naturally have strong ideas about how you want it to be styled and worn on the catwalk. Remember, though, that a student show is a vehicle for a large number of people and that it is not possible to mastermind it as if it were a production for a single designer. Colleges have limited funds, and while most will try to take account of individual students' wishes, it is necessary to streamline the use of models. You may have some choice over the casting of models for type, colouring and height and also over music and accessories.

Not all fashion-college programmes feel it is appropriate to test or showcase their students on the runway. There are many aspects of fashion design that do not lend themselves to this form of exposure. All fashion courses, however, stress the importance of having a good, professional-looking portfolio over the momentary spectacle of the catwalk. The colleges usually hold an exhibition of end-of-year work to which interested parties and manufacturers are invited. Increasingly, courses are looking to new technologies, such as digital video and the internet, to help students to promote themselves more widely.

### Tips for styling your college show

Try to keep your concept simple. A clear silhouette, colour and design message come across most effectively if it is not overwhelmed by styling tricks or models who look vastly different from one another.

Visualize the effect you want. Do you want your models to appear singly, in pairs or as a group; to walk fast or slow; to take items off or pose?

Tell your tutors what you plan to do well in advance – you will lose marks for last-minute theatricals. A show with some unusual features as high points can work well, provided it is organized in advance and planned into the running order for maximum effect.

Graduate shows are often held in temporary exhibition sites.

Even at student shows there is a hierarchy of seating, and security is necessary.

The crowd gathers outside.

Models who are not professional – however beautiful or beloved – can often spoil the presentation by being in the wrong place, walking badly or self-consciously or attempting to upstage one another. Rehearse them so that you can spot and iron out any idiosyncrasies.

Models have their own ideas about what they are prepared to wear. A few will refuse to wear very short or revealing garments; others will baulk at putting on an outfit they think makes them look foolish or ugly. Be diplomatic: swap outfits around; if all else fails, cry! It is necessary for models to change their outfits very fast between 'runs'. Beware of using complicated accessories – tights (pantyhose), belts and jewellery all take time to put on and remove. Change times need to be checked or the flow of the show may grind to a halt. You may have to beg, borrow, hire or put down expensive deposits on accessories and items for the show. Organize this well in advance.

Show producers usually have a team of professional dressers. You may not be allowed backstage to check that everything is perfect just before it hits the runway. It is important to have drawings and lists of what goes with what and how each outfit is to be worn. Make sure the dresser and the models understand what is expected. Have extra pairs of tights or pantyhose at the ready as these can be ruined or lost in rehearsals. Attach or pin on any accessories that can be fixed to garments. Undo and explain complicated fastenings on clothes to the dresser. Some 'conceptual' fashion will need demonstrating to both model and dresser.

If you want elaborate hairstyles, don't forget that the necks of your garments must go easily and quickly over heads. Some colleges insist on a simple, sleek hairstyle throughout the show. It is possible to style this with wigs and hats, but take care – nothing will look more foolish than a slipping hairpiece. You may have to compromise with a make-up style that suits all students unless you have your own models or are the last to use a 'set' of models and they have time to apply extra effects between changes.

If you are borrowing shoes or having them made, find out the models' shoe sizes. Most tall models have larger-than-average feet. It can be useful to pick a style that is adjustable or where a bad fit does not show: for example, slingbacks, boots and brogues (Oxfords). Contact the suppliers well in advance and make sure the shoes are there in plenty of time before the show so that the models can try

The dresser has a moment of peace before the show.

The press arrive early. The show will be videotaped for the exhibition.

A student anxiously checks her outfits before they go on the runway.

them on and be comfortable walking in them. Cover the soles of the shoes in masking tape to stop them from being marked and non-returnable. Simple choices such as flip-flops are cheap, stylish, easy and understated.

You will probably be allowed to select your own music track for your collection. You will be given a finite length of time, so make sure that the track is neither too long nor too short. Start listening to potential choices at least a month beforehand, and try 'walking' to the music. Highly monotonous, loud or atonal avant-garde music can irritate more than please.

Special effects can heighten your designs, but if done badly, they can be disastrous. Dry ice, for example, can make an audience suffer from coughing and sore eyes or obliterate the clothes completely. Health and safety regulations may not allow what you have in mind so check these before hiring any expensive equipment. Showers of water, glitter, thrown flowers or 'accompaniments' such as dogs are best left to the finale or models will be stepping in debris left on the runway throughout the show. After the show collect any accessories quickly. It can be chaotic backstage, and small items can be damaged or lost.

'It's all over very quickly. You study for three or four years and then it's all over in three or four minutes …' Final-year student

**Above** The impact of the runway line-up allows the audience to see the silhouette and colour together.

**Opposite** The show ends with a dramatic show-stopper.

# Student exhibitions

A commonly required part of the fashion and textile academic degree is a small exhibition of your final project and portfolio to assist in the assessment of your work. Over the years these assessment shows have grown into delightful exhibitions, which are initially just for parents and invited luminaries but which are later opened to the public, sometimes for a fee. The standard of display and presentation skills is very high, and much of it must be planned well in advance.

You are often given only a day or so to prepare the stand and put up your element of the show; any special fittings, lighting and shelving must be discussed beforehand with college staff. Photography, graphics and elaborate slide shows or video pieces should all be organized weeks ahead. If you are required to show your garments, make sure that they have hangers that complement them. Clothing will be less likely to go missing and looks more professional if you put on name tags and swing-ticket labels. The graphics for these and your business cards should have an overall identity that helps someone to remember your work. Textile swatches can also be headed with the same information and displayed in a way that makes them enticing to handle. There is usually a shelf or cradle for your portfolio.

Try and transmit your personality, but beware of cluttering up the display – the smaller the space, the simpler it should be. Sketchbooks and technical work should be piled up neatly for the assessment but they are often removed before the show opens to the public for reasons of space and security. You are usually expected to be present at times during the exhibition in order to keep your area safe and tidy, answer enquiries and promote your work and that of others. After the exhibition, follow up on any enquiries that have been made, reorganize your portfolio and start looking for your first job.

## Graduate showcases

Most fashion and textile degree courses also belong to associations for showcasing their students' work to industry. Graduate fashion-design exhibitions are an excellent opportunity for making contacts, getting feedback about your work and also seeing and learning from the work of others. Prestigious prizes are awarded by a panel of sponsors and industry observers, and the shows are attended by the press, television, fashion scouts and designers. This is not a time to relax; you must be there and on your best behaviour if you wish to stand a chance among the many hundreds of hopeful talents.

**Opposite** If they have been helping backstage, students do not see the impact of their collections on the runway until they watch the video playback.

**Top** At some colleges only the best examples of student work are put on display.

**Above** TV and press interview the students whose work has caught their eye.

**Overleaf, left** Some colleges reserve large exhibition spaces so that all their students can display their designs equally.

**Overleaf, right** An accessory collection is well displayed at eye level.

# Your portfolio

It is essential to have a professional display portfolio from the very start as a way of keeping designs and artwork flat, orderly and portable. If you can afford to do so, buy two – one for carrying about day to day, one to use for interviews. An A1 (84.1 x 59.4 cm, 33 x 23$^{1}/_{2}$ in) portfolio is appropriate only if you have excellent large-scale work; otherwise it is easier to travel with an A2 (59.4 x 42 cm, 23$^{1}/_{2}$ x 16$^{1}/_{2}$ in) or A3 (42 x 29.7 cm, 16$^{1}/_{2}$ x 11$^{3}/_{4}$ in) portfolio. Avoid carrying bulky work or sketchbooks; although these may be interesting, they do not look professional. Photocopy any especially good pages and put them in the portfolio.

The central spine of spring clips holds transparent sleeves; this makes it faster to rearrange. Estimate how many pages you need. A portfolio that is too empty or too full can look amateurish. It is a good idea to sort your work into order and lay out all the pages before you slip them into the plastic sleeves. Think about which work will appear on right-hand pages as there is a tendency for people to pay more attention to these.

In some colleges you may be expected to put work into chronological order for assessment purposes. However, for maximum visual effect you should sort your work into best, secondary and 'maybe' piles of projects; edit these and arrange them as if they were articles in a magazine, with the most eye-catching work at the start, following on with good work and tailing off towards the end. Finish with a strong 'conversation piece'. Try and keep the orientation of all the pages the same. It is very tiring to have to keep moving your head or turn the whole portfolio around to view the designs. Don't clutter up your pages; you will be familiar with your work, but others will be seeing your portfolio for the first time and it will just confuse them. Each section should tell the story of how you went about researching, creating design developments and resolving the brief.

Make a decision as to the overall layout and style. The book should feel like the work of one person and show up your strengths, not your weaknesses. Sleeves often come with a sheet of black backing paper that can set off your own artwork well. It is not a good idea to change the background colour too often. Neutrals are usually smartest, but too much black can have a depressing effect. Use the paper that comes in the sleeve as a size guide and trim other papers to this size.

Keep the effect uncluttered by including a border around your work. Glue only the corners of the artwork down, as you may want to move it in the future. Loose or light fixing allows you to reposition pieces. Not everything looks good in transparent sleeves; the polythene can dull vibrant colours. If you have made beautiful fabrics, it may be better if they can be freely handled.

Each project should be clearly defined; titles will help to make it clear what each section is about. Make sure you write on a separate piece of paper, not directly onto the artwork. It is embarrassing to be told by your interviewer that you have spelt something wrong, so check everything carefully. Handwriting can look relaxed, but it will look more professional if it is done on a computer. Keep notes and titles short, but write enough to give an idea as to what was intended should you have to leave the portfolio with someone. Do not put dates on the work as it can make the work look passé.

Collages of research work can look good as an introduction to a project, but if the pieces on them are bulky it is best to get them colour-photocopied. Curiously, colour copies sometimes look better than the original artwork. Some people like to laser-copy their entire portfolio, as an archive and also for continuity, although this can lead the interviewer to doubt that the work originates with you. Large drawings can look neater if reduced, and bringing sketches down to one size can add a more professional uniformity. The portfolio should contain a balance of clear and considered drawings with some roughs or finished illustrations that show more artistic spirit. Vary the number of figures in a layout and the scale and media with which they are produced. You should aim to show a variety of work and styles that indicate your versatility designing for different seasons and colour palettes.

Check the order by looking through it a number of times to see how it reads – it should have features that keep you turning the pages. It can be useful to have

**Left** Portfolios are laid out for people in the industry to browse through.

**Top** Knitwear is difficult to display yet tempting to touch.

**Above** Your garments will be examined closely for style, cut, fabric, finish and colour.

a dramatic fold-out presentation piece to pull out of the portfolio sleeve if the conversation starts to lag as well as a copy of an illustration that you can leave behind with your business card as a memory-jogger.

There are other ways of presenting work. You can show slides on a portable light box, or you could make a digital portfolio and résumé to hand over as a CD-ROM. Do not put all of your best work on this, but do include something memorable and significant.

When applying for a particular job, your portfolio should be organized to maximize your appeal. Research the company, find out what it has produced in recent seasons and its marketing objectives. Go through your work and review it in the light of who will be looking at it.

# Your first job

There are a great many unrealistic perceptions of the glamour of working in fashion. The final shows set the adrenalin flowing and hopes are high, but you should be prepared for disappointment. Only a lucky few are plucked from their college degree exhibitions and set on a glittering path. When you do find employment, you may have to start at the bottom, work hard and make slow progress to reach your goal. Thinking through where you want to work and why you are pursuing a career in fashion will help you decide wisely how to approach the stages of the ladder. It is often better to accept a lower-paid job with a well-respected company that offers training and wider opportunities than a narrow but highly paid short-term position. Entry-level jobs may not satisfy your desire to design, but they will teach you basic background skills and responsibility and will look good on your CV.

### The work placement or internship

For a graduate, sudden exposure to the world of work can be daunting. It need not be, however, and the key here is preparation. Start networking early in your college career, find work experience or take a placement. At the very least you

**Right** The press room at Graduate Fashion Week.

**Opposite** If you visit the stands during Graduate Fashion Week, you can see what the colleges have to offer.

can try finding holiday jobs with a company that interests you. Some colleges offer sandwich courses, which include a sustained period of work experience within the industry as part of, or in addition to, the curriculum. This is called a placement, or internship. This is a very useful way to test out and view at first hand the different career paths and roles available.

Although placement work is often not well-remunerated, the experience should prove a valuable investment. Usually you will be taken on in the position of a studio junior. Typical tasks may include everything from modelling toiles (muslins) and sewing on labels and buttons to answering the phone, making the coffee and running out for sandwiches. You are unlikely to be asked to design or contribute to the collection while on a placement, but if you are alert you will be given more complex jobs and responsibility as you prove your competence.

Your personality and self-presentation will be under scrutiny in these circumstances; you can be easily replaced. Timekeeping and orderliness, hard work and good manners are valued. Contacts and friends can be made who will form part of your future network and who may be willing to give you references or sponsorship in funds or in kind. Many students are asked back to work after they graduate, in the much more rewarding role of junior designer.

> 'I had the most wonderful time on my placement. I was really nervous when I first started and didn't dare speak to the designers, but everyone was so friendly that I soon got into it. The best part was helping out at the collections and seeing it all come together and knowing which bits I'd had a hand in. Now I know my way around Paris, too. I feel really sophisticated.' Third-year student

Your college will usually ask you to write an evaluative report on the structure of the company, the nature of its products and the tasks that you were given. It is a good idea to keep a work diary and to ask your colleagues for information and material that you can use in your report. Your employer may also be asked to fill in a form or give a verbal account of your conduct in the workplace.

If you finish your collection in good time,
you can improve on your presentation with
a photo shoot.

# Careers in fashion

The creative-design world thrives on networking and contacts, and many of the top jobs are never advertised. Word may go out to some select agencies, but most design positions are filled from recommendations, sometimes from college tutors, from previous contact through freelance work, or by poaching or headhunting staff from competitors. Increasingly, the creative fields are cutting back on permanent core staff positions and looking instead for contract workers with the skills or design style in vogue at the time. The fashion industry is notorious for the lack of secure positions. The maxim 'you're only as good as your last collection' haunts all designers.

There are, however, a wide number of career opportunities besides that of designer that offer scope for your creativity, skill and knowledge. Some are technical jobs, others involve statistics and logistics, and some have a high social aspect, involving liaison with press and public. It is a varied field. There is full-time, part-time and a great deal of freelance and consultancy work. There are too many levels of career and variations on a theme within fashion to list them all, but below is a broad guide to the areas of employment that you might consider.

## Manufacturing

Fashion manufacturing companies (see Chapter II) require fashion-oriented and fashion-trained individuals to steer their production, market their wares and to liaise between their customers and the manufacturing process. Fashion designers with technical knowledge of fabric printing, weaving or knitting expertise are well-placed to work closely with the manufacturing industry. Fabric companies and fibre and knitwear manufacturers frequently employ fashion designers and stylists to organize and coordinate their ranges, and to stage showroom and trade exhibitions to promote their merchandise. Fashion manufacturers that make garments for 'own-label' stores and chains also require personable and well-presented sales staff, who can often earn more than buyers or designers. Many designers find their first jobs within manufacturing: as assistant pattern-cutters, production assistants or sample machinists. These positions are reasonably well-paid, highly instructional and satisfying ways of entering the industry.

## Buying and retail

The fashion buyer may be the owner or employee of a single boutique or a member of a very large store team. Stores and chains subdivide their merchandise categories so buyers specialize in a single field or market sector of product, such as ladies' knitwear or eveningwear. There are two main ways of operating: centralized and departmental buying.

Centralized buying allows chains to move stock from shop to shop; large quantities can also mean negotiable price reductions. Departmental buying is more local. Buyers are usually accountable to the fashion director, who will indicate the overall buying policy but usually allow the buyer to make decisions as to the content of an order. To join a professional store buying team, you will either have worked your way up from a junior position as a sales assistant or have a fashion training with marketing skills and enter as an assistant buyer. Considerable shop-floor experience is essential before reaching this glamorous and well-paid pinnacle of retail as it requires you to perform a skilful balancing act between creative instinct for customer desires and good commercial practice.

Press and celebrities mix with the help of the fashion PR. Here, Plum Sykes of UK *Vogue* poses with actress Minnie Driver.

The buyer must keep abreast of what is actually selling and what is appearing in the magazines and be able to predict customer demand six months to a year ahead. Many designers actively court the attentions of buyers by inviting them to parties and giving them preferential seating at shows. The buyer is in a position to give tactful feedback to the designer about how to improve a range as well as how to promote his or her work. The buyer is expected to make between two and twelve marketing trips a year, and much of his or her time will also be spent viewing collections in showrooms or taking appointments from salespeople. A buyer needs to convey a sense of maturity and look professional and businesslike; creative vision, a head for figures and diplomacy in handling juniors and managerial staff and designers are all desirable attributes.

## Merchandising

This vague term is sometimes applied to the buying and mixing of stock. More correctly, however, it denotes the job of financial arrangement that lies behind the buyer's tasks. A merchandiser will authorize mark-downs and discounts for multiple purchases or move them to another branch. Merchandisers are experts at shop layout and distribution of goods and work in close collaboration with buyers. Because the title is also used rather loosely for a sales assistant with responsibility for the arrangement of stock on the shop floor, it is important when applying for a position in merchandising to ask for a clear job description. Good organizational skills and a talent for numbers are needed for this post.

## Fashion public relations

Fashion companies are often too busy to do the promotion of their designs themselves so they use the services of a public-relations (PR) company to publicize them. The PR company's job is to generate buzz about a collection and it is responsible for making connections with magazines, TV, newspapers and radio stations. Getting the right mix of people to attend the shows – fashion editors, buyers and stars – can make the difference between creating a newsworthy event and a fashion flop.

To work in PR you need literacy and journalistic skills; you must be articulate and able to provide the press with an off-the-cuff sound bite or advise designers as to how to handle publicity should something untoward or dramatic occur. Personality is important. PRs are 'people persons' – at ease in social situations and good at smoothing the friction between diverse individuals. Understanding the hierarchies of seating arrangements at shows, schmoozing and partying, being chatty and up front are key skills in this job. Being well-connected and well-dressed can help, too. A significant proportion of the work will take place at evening events, and a considerable amount of travelling is often required.

## Fashion journalism

The fashion media is a most effective way of getting designers noticed, and the fashion journalist consequently can wield a great deal of power. Writers such as Colin McDowell for the British *Sunday Times*, Suzy Menkes for the *International Herald Tribune*, and American *Vogue* editor Anna Wintour hold some of the most respected positions in the fashion industry. It is the job of the fashion journalist to attend the shows and exhibitions, and to analyse and comment on the trends and news for public consumption. Journalists are much courted by the fashion companies, who shower them with goods and give them front-row seats in the hope that reviews will be favourable.

The journalists' duty is to interpret the designs and broad changes in fashion, not only with their own well-practised eye but with a view to the readership and the advertisers who support their magazine. Fashion journalists will be under pressure for deadlines and must come up with hot stories and angles on the same shows that hundreds of other journalists have seen. Between the fashion-show seasons they may be expected to contribute to weekly planning meetings and come up with stories and ideas to keep the public interest.

Fashion journalism has expanded in recent years to include scriptwriting and presentation on television and cable programmes with magazine formats and style content. Today you must have desktop-publishing (DTP) and word-processing skills and are expected to file copy by telecommunications.

## Fashion stylist

A fashion stylist works closely with the fashion magazines and photographers. A stylist is not a designer but an interpreter of fashion who puts together the looks for a photographic shoot – either as interpretations of what the editor has ordered or off his or her own back. Sometimes people are surprised that the best stylists are not among the youngest operators. Taste and style are timeless languages, and, like costume designers, the stylist calls on a vast, absorbed knowledge of clothing ideas that 'work'. Moreover, in a time-pressured industry, efficiency and experience are worthwhile attributes that grow with you.

Stylists often have a creative relationship with a particular editor or photographer that establishes a personal rapport and a look. Others work with designers to help them crystallize the look for their fashion shows. For many years, Amanda Grieve was the stylist for John Galliano, and Katy England styles for Alexander McQueen. Magazines often use an in-house stylist to give a continuity of approach to their regular pages. The stylist can have great impact on the way that we dress and our bearing, but the job is one of the least visible in the fashion media. Stylists are not usually college-trained, and the job normally requires a long and poorly paid apprenticeship working with magazines and catalogues or assisting a photographer.

## Fashion photography

Fashion photography is a specialized branch of the magazine and graphics industry. For those with exceptional talent, it can be a lucrative and glamorous life. It is a very fast-paced and pressured job, and work must be turned out to publishing requirements and deadlines. Most photographers are freelance and self-employed. They often have agents who take enquiries and show their work to potential clients. There is considerable initial outlay on equipment, studio and travel, which may not be recouped until a much later date. Photographers are generally commissioned and will discuss with the fashion editor what is required of them. Only when they have become significantly well-known can they produce and market editorial shots that they have initiated.

Being a fashion photographer is an arduous and sometimes quite lonely occupation. There is more time spent in the darkroom developing and printing than is popularly imagined, but there are also opportunities for travel to exotic locations in the company of beautiful people, all expenses paid. Photographers

**Top** Fashion journalists tread the line between amusing their public and offending or praising the designers. Isabella Blow, fashion stylist and Colin McDowell, journalist and author.

**Above** Fashion photography is a competitive and time-pressured job.

often work with a small team of assistants, stylists and make-up artists who work together to realize a fashion look. Catwalk photographers specialize in covering the shows and have to be ruthless about maintaining their rank in the hierarchy and getting the right shots back to base. Catalogue and newspaper photographers work on assignments. To become a fashion photographer you need technical camera skills, but more important is a creative eye and an understanding of lighting, fashion and the ability to live with a near-constant adrenalin rush.

### Prediction and forecasting

Prediction companies, or bureaus, offer a forecasting and reporting service to the fashion industry (see p.94). They research the trends that might feed into the industry and put together bias-free information reports that they sell to the larger companies. Prediction companies work approximately eighteen months to two years ahead. The larger consultancies employ a team of in-house designers to illustrate current fashions, analyse details and draw up variations on a theme. The standards of work and quality of information is high and the cost of putting together the reports is expensive. The client expects a lot of versatility and up-to-date information.

Prediction company account executives work closely with a group of clients and also travel to the trade fairs and fashion centres that are of interest to them. They are involved with commissioning artwork and photography from creatives and write reports and statistical analyses. If you enjoy travel and the social scene, you might start on this career ladder by offering your services as a trendspotter.

# Writing a CV or résumé

Whatever your chosen career path, getting your CV (curriculum vitae) and portfolio right from the start will give you a strong advantage. Because of the nature of the academic year, thousands of new graduates arrive on the job market at the same time, so you need to have an edge. A CV is a summary of your skills, accomplishments and education designed to capture a potential employer's interest and secure an interview. It should be no more than two pages long. A short covering letter explaining why you are applying should also be included. Below are a few guidelines to bear in mind while compiling your CV.

Write your CV on a computer. It can be easily edited or updated, and looks smart.
Don't be tempted to use fancy typefaces. Keep it clear, concise and legible.
Use only the name that you are actually known by on your CV.
Present educational and employment information in reverse chronological order.
Don't list all of your academic qualifications and grades, only the relevant ones.

List any honours, awards and exhibitions. Never lie about qualifications or experience; you will be found out.
List skills such as languages and computer training and whether or not you hold a driving licence.
Don't give names and phone numbers of references. You can put 'references available on request' at the bottom of the page.

Leave out photos and personal data such as marital status, health, religion, ethnicity and commonplace recreational activities.

List any positions of responsibility. Don't state how much you have earned on previous jobs or your salary requirements.

Have someone proofread your CV for typos and other errors.

Always make sure that you approach the right contact in the company.

Always tailor your CV and portfolio to the job for which you are applying.

If you can, include a letter of recommendation or reference from a tutor or previous employer.

A single page of illustration or a postcard-style business card can be eye-catching if relevant to the position.

Follow up your CV with a phone call about two weeks later to see whether it is under consideration and if you can make an appointment for an interview.

# The interview – some dos and don'ts

Do some homework on the company so that you have a reasonable idea of its history, product line and market.

Make sure you know exactly where to go and arrive in plenty of time so that you are not hot and flustered. You are likely to be nervous, so quietly collect your thoughts and run over the key things that you would like to say or ask your interviewer about the company or job.

How you dress will make an impression, but don't overdo it. Wearing one of your own creations is appropriate, providing it is not out of place. Do not smoke or chew gum or make jokes. Try not to fiddle with your hair or fidget. Good posture and good body language will demonstrate confidence.

Be honest about your skills and back up your strengths with examples from your portfolio. Some companies will be prepared to give you training in specialist areas, so do not pretend you can do things that you cannot.

A friendly, flexible and persevering demeanour can work wonders. There is a fine line between confidence and arrogance. Look upon any job as an opportunity to learn and develop new skills and talents. Smile and make eye contact.

Ask about aspects of the job that you do not understand or which have not been mentioned, such as working hours and the number of people to whom you would report. Ask how the job could develop in the future. It is not wise to appear too eager to discuss wages; pick your moment. Don't, however, accept the job without knowing the financial package.

Don't appear either too cool or too desperate. Even if you have other job offers, do not talk about these at length. The company will want to hear that you are interested in them primarily.

Do not leave your portfolio behind to be looked at later by someone who is absent. Always make another appointment. Not all companies are honest.

If you are not successful on this occasion, don't be disheartened. An ability to bounce back and believe in yourself and the skills you have worked hard to achieve will be recognized sooner or later.

Only a talented and dedicated few will make it to the ranks of designers with their own labels. Matthew Williamson takes a bow with Helena Christensen.

Whether graduating from your fashion course is marked by a fanfare of shows, exhibitions and ceremonies or the arrival of your certificate by post, it will be a moment of great personal pride. The acknowledgement of a rite of passage that has taken years of hard work, but has also brought you valuable creative and practical skills, friendships and fun indicates that you are ready to embark upon the first steps of a career that will be engrossing, rewarding and ever changing. Good luck!

# Glossary

**Apparel** Another term for clothing; most commonly used in the USA.

**Assessment** The process of formal evaluation and awarding marks for design work.

**Atelier** A fashion studio. Parisian ateliers are designated either as *flou* (for dressmaking) or *tailleur* (for tailoring suits and coats).

**Avant-garde** A fashion or concept that is ahead of its time.

**Bespoke** Individual made-to-measure tailoring for men's suits.

**Bias** The crossgrain or 45 degree angle when the weft is folded to the warp.

**Blocks** A set of basic individual or standard-sized pattern templates from which designs can be developed. Blocks are known as slopers in the USA.

**Bottom weights** The heavier weight fabrics used for skirts and trousers.

**Boutique** French word for an independent, usually small shop with unique stock and atmosphere.

**Brainstorming** Open discussion among colleagues to bring up new ideas and concepts.

**Brand** A name or trademark used to identify a product and denote quality, value or a particular ethos.

**Bridge fashion** An American term for clothing placed between designer fashion and high-street style.

**Buyer** The person responsible for planning, buying and selling merchandise.

**Buying office** The department responsible for buying within a store, or an independent body that arranges to buy for chains and boutiques, especially from overseas suppliers.

**Cabbage** The term given to unused fabric or garments made from over-supply of fabric for manufacturing.

**CAD/CAM** Computer-aided design and computer-aided manufacturing.

**Capsule collection** A small range of related designs with a special purpose or impact.

**Chain stores** A group of stores, usually in high-street locations, which are centrally owned, operated and merchandised to sell under the same logo with a distinctive and recognizable product.

**Classic** A term for a style that remains constantly popular and changes very little in detail; for example, men's shirts, jeans.

**Cognoscenti** Italian word for 'those in the know', i.e. fashion aware.

**Collection** The term used for a group of better quality fashion clothes with related features or intended for a specific season. 'The Collections' is a colloquial way of indicating the Paris fashion shows.

**Colourway** The name for the limited range of colours that may be offered in a style or collection and also for the choice of colours available in a printed textile.

**Concession** A leased use of department store space to sell another company's goods.

**Conglomerate** A financial parent organization that owns a number of companies which may not be related in terms of product or target market.

**Consumer** The end user or buyer of a product.

**Conversationals** Printed fabrics with unusual prints, such as Hawaiian shirts, animals etc.

**Converter** A manufacturer who makes raw fibre into fabric or converts greige goods into printed fabric.

**Coordinates** Fabrics or items of clothing that relate in colour or style and are intended to be worn together.

**Costing sheets** A list detailing the time and cost of materials and processes used in making a garment.

**Couturier** French word for fashion designer.

**Critique/crit** Discussion and evaluation of work, often held as a group session at the end of a project or assignment.

**Croquis** A line drawing made by the designer to illustrate a garment or a painted design for a printed fabric.

**Cruise** A period immediately after the Winter holidays when 'cruise' or resort wear is sold in the USA.

**Deconstruction** A style of designing which originated with Belgian designers, whereby garments were left rough and unfinished or revealed construction details.

**Degree show** The exhibition of work which is displayed and assessed to ascertain a student's degree classification.

**Demi-couture** High-end fashion, often the diffusion range of a couturier.

**Demographics** A marketing term for determining the distribution of statistics relating to a market segment, e.g. age, gender, income, lifestyle and housing.

**Design developments** Drawings that progress through desirable or successful elements within a design theme.

**Diffusion range** A line of clothing that is a secondary or lower-priced and simplified version of a designer collection.

**Distance learning** Assignments and practical work done off campus, usually through the medium of a computer.

**Docket** The paperwork for the manufacturer's order for clothing.

**Draping** A method of making a fashion style or pattern by manipulating fabric on a body or dress form.

**EPOS** Electronic point-of-sale is the term used when the till is linked to a computer network, often with barcode scanners.

**E-zines** Internet magazine formats and news exchanges.

**Fabrication** The manufacturing detail and content of a material used for fashion.

**Fad** A very short-lived fashion.

**Fascia** The company logo, as shown on a shop front or display material.

**Fashion cycle** The calendar by which a company will plan, design, make and market its ranges.

**Final collection** The last college collection before graduation.

**Findings** A term for the trimmings or notions that are included on a style, e.g. buttons and lace.

**Flats** Diagrammatic drawings.

**Focus group** A marketing group who are asked their opinions in order to fine tune or get feedback on a product or market sector.

**Franchise, franchisee** A licensing system allowing individuals to sell goods.

**Fusible fabrics** Heat-sensitive fabrics which bond with other materials to strengthen them.

**Geometrics** Printed fabrics with lines, spots, squares or similar non-organic designs.

**Glossies** The high-quality magazines.

**Grading** A process of mathematically sizing up a garment pattern to a range of fittings.

**Grain** Straight grain bias.

**Greige goods** (pronounced grey) Fabric in its basic unfinished state, e.g. unbleached calico.

**Grunge** An anti-fashion style of designing or combining clothing to look deliberately poor, ill-fitting or mismatched.

**Hand/handle** The feel of a fabric.

**Handwriting, signature** Your personal designing style, design features or way of drawing.

**Haute couture** French term for the highest quality of dressmaking. A designer or company cannot call themselves *haute couture* unless they have passed the stringent criteria of the Chambre Syndical of the Fédération Française de la Couture.

**Industrial placement** Also known as internship or temporary work experience.

**Interlining** A fabric which is placed between the garment fabric and lining as a strengthening or padding material.

**JIT** Just-in-time, a way of manufacturing quickly in response to consumer demand.

**Jobber** A person or company that buys fabric from mills or manufacturers to resell to companies who do not require large quantities of cloth or cannot afford the minimum wholesale lengths.

**Kimball** A system for tagging clothes with tickets.

**Knock off** A copy of a designer or desirable garment made with inferior fabric and trimmings and sold at a lower price.

**Lab-dips** Colour tests on swatches of fabric or yarn.

**Label** The tag which identifies the designer or manufacturer and the origin, fibre contents and wash care of the product. Sometimes used synonymously with logo.

**Layout pad** A sketchbook with thin sheets of paper which can be traced through.

**Lay plan** Also known as a marker, this is the template for cutting the pattern from the fabric to ensure as little waste as possible.

**Licensing** The authorization by contract for the use of a name, logo or product type to be used by another manufacturing company in exchange for royalty payments.

**Light fast/colour fast** The degree of permanence of a dye colour to light or washing.

**Line** A term used to denote styles related in theme and detail. In the USA it is synonymous with the European use of the word collection.

**Line-for-line copy** An exact copy of a style, sometimes licensed but more often illegal.

**Line-up** A preview of toiles or finished garments on models to determine the balance, range and order in a collection.

**Logo** A brand name or symbol used to identify a product or designer.

**Loss leader** A style sold at less than the usual mark-up in order to attract buyers to other designs.

**Mark-up** The difference between the cost price and the selling price, including taxes.

**Mood board** A presentation board which gives the overall concept and direction of a design collection.

**Multifibre Arrangement (MFA)** An international agreement among importing and exporting nations to prevent import surges and regulate trade.

**Muslin** *see* Toile

**Off-price** Bargain goods sold at lower than the original wholesale price.

**Off-schedule** A fashion show that is not on the official show organizers list.

**Off-shore production** Manufacturing abroad.

**Outworker** An individual who makes up garments for a factory or designer from their home.

**Over-dyeing/cross-dyeing** Fabrics may require more than one application of dye to colour different fibre types and give depth to a material.

**Palette** A range or gamut of colours used in a collection.

**Pattern drafting, pattern cutting, pattern making** The drawing out of a flat pattern from measurements or through the use of block templates.

**Piece work** The method of making a garment by handing it down a line of machinists who each carry out a different function.

**Portfolio** A large portable container for flat artwork and press cuttings that should give a potential client a comprehensive view of the designer's capabilities.

**Première Vision** Also known as P.V. French for 'first look' and the name of the major fabric trade fair held twice a year in Paris.

*Prêt-à-porter* French for ready-to-wear, a term used for better quality and designer separates, also the name of a major fashion exhibition.

**Price point** Different ranges of price indicate quality and market level, e.g. budget, designer, luxury.

**Private label** Companies often use their spare manufacturing capacity to make garments for stores and other companies who will put their own label in the garments.

**Proportion** The relationship and balance of one aspect of a design with another, a principle of fashion design.

**Quotas** The international trade in fabrics is limited by governments with a quota system to prevent their markets being flooded with cheap goods.

**Ready-to-wear** Also known as off-the peg, *prêt-à-porter*; clothing separates.

**Retail** The selling of goods from a business to an individual consumer.

**Roughs** First-stage drawings for designs, usually quickly made in pencil and without extraneous detail.

**Salon/showroom** A place or office where salespersons show a collection or merchandise to potential buyers.

**Sample** A test garment (also known as a toile or muslin) made from calico or inferior fabric.

**Sample cut** A short length of fabric used to make up a sample garment.

**Sealing sample** The garment that serves as the approved standard to which all others must be made.

**Selvedges** The edges of the woven fabric that are parallel to the warp.

**Separates** Individual items of clothing.

**Short run** A small manufacturing order for clothes.

**Silhouette** The overall shape of a garment or of a collection reduced to a basic geometric or alphanumeric description, e.g. boxy, A-line, figure-8.

**Source book, look book** Forecast reports available within the industry.

**Sourcing** The search for materials, trimmings and manufacturing at the best prices and delivery times.

**Specification sheet** Also known as specs. A technical design drawing including measurements and manufacturing details such as stitching and trimmings.

**Staple** The length of a basic fibre such as wool or cashmere, these are spun together to make a continuous thread.

**Stories** Design themes comprising fabric, colour or style associations used within a collection.

**Storyboard** Also known as a theme board, a presentation of the concept for a collection with the breakdown of styles and coordinates detailed.

**Stylist** A fashion expert who prepares fashion items for photographs or presentations.

**Tear sheets** Also known as swipes, these are pictures taken from magazines, etc., which are used as initial inspiration or corroboration for a concept, not to copy.

**Toile** Literally, the French for a lightweight muslin but used to describe a sample or test garment.

**Trademark** A logo or brand that has been protected or copyrighted by registration.

**Transitional** The period in between seasons when the weather is uncertain and styles overlap due to the demands of the public and the need for fresh merchandise.

**Trimming** A term used both for the decorative detail on a garment and for the process of finishing and cutting (cleaning) loose threads.

**Tutorial** A discussion with teaching staff to discuss progress.

**UPC** Universal product codes, standard codes on price tags which allow data to be read electronically at stocktaking or point-of-sale.

**USP** Unique selling point. That which differentiates a designer or company style.

**Vendor** Supplier or person who sells goods.

**Virtual catwalk** Computer-aided visualization of a fashion show using digitally-generated figures and clothing.

**Visual diary** A sketchbook worked over the period of a project to show developing ideas.

**Warp/weft** The warp threads of a woven fabric are those that comprise the lengthwise grain. The weft threads are placed in by shuttle at 90 degrees to the warp and run from selvedge to selvedge giving the fabric its width.

**Wholesale** The selling of goods from business to business, usually in bulk quantity and with terms and conditions which may include discounts and credit.

**Yoke** A piece of fabric used to support a fuller or gathered length, e.g. across the shoulders of a shirt or from the hipline of a skirt.

*Zeitgeist* A German word for 'spirit of the times' often used in conjunction with fashion as clothing reflects the era of its creation.

# Further reading

**Chapter I**
Roland Barthes, *The Fashion System*, Paris, 1967
Peter York, *Style Wars*, London, Sidgwick & Jackson, 1980

**Chapter II**
Teri Agins, *The End of Fashion*, New York, William Morrow and Co., 1999
Nicholas Coleridge, *The Fashion Conspiracy*, London, Heinemann, 1988
Colin McDowell, *The Designer Scam*, London, Random House, 1994
Hugh Sebag-Montefiore, *Kings on the Catwalk*, London, Chapmans, 1992

**Chapter III**
Bina Abling, *Fashion Rendering with Color*, New York, Prentice Hall, 2001
Anne Allen and Julian Seaman, *Fashion Drawing: The Basic Principles*, London, Batsford, 1996
Laird Borelli, *Fashion Illustration Now*, London, Thames & Hudson, 2000
Janet Boyes, *Essential Fashion Design: Illustration Theme Boards, Body Coverings, Projects, Portfolios*, London, Batsford, 1997
Yajima Isao, *Fashion Illustration in Europe*, Tokyo, Graphic-Sha, 1988
Kojiro Kumagai, *Fashion Illustration: Expressing Textures*, Tokyo, Graphic-Sha, 1988
Alice Mackrell, *An Illustrated History of Fashion: 500 Years of Fashion Illustration*, New York, Costume and Fashion Press, 1997
Julian Seaman, *Professional Fashion Illustration*, London, Batsford, 1995
Steven Stipelman, *Illustrating Fashion: Concept to Creation*, New York, Fairchild, 1996
Sharon Lee Tate, *The Complete Book of Fashion Illustration*, New Jersey, Prentice Hall, 1996

**Chapter IV**
Faber Birren, *The Textile Colorist*, New York, Van Nostrand Reinhold, 1980
S. E. Braddock and M. O'Mahony, *Techno Textiles: Revolutionary Fabrics for Fashion & Design*, London, Thames & Hudson, 1998
Chlöe Colchester, *The New Textiles: Trends and Traditions*, London, Thames & Hudson, 1991
Gill Dalby, *Natural Dyes – Fast or Fugitive*, Ashill Publications, 1992
J. Feltwell, *The Story of Silk*, Gloucestershire, Alan Sutton, 1990
Simon Garfield, *Mauve*, London, Faber & Faber, 2000
Susannah Handley, *Nylon: The Manmade Fashion Revolution*, London, Bloomsbury, 1999
Johannes Itten, *The Elements of Colour*, New York, Van Nostrand Reinhold, 1982

Ezio Manzini, *The Material of Invention*, Cambridge, Mass., MIT Press, 1989
Deborah Newton, *Designing Knitwear*, Newtown, CT, Taunton Press, 1992
Mary Schoeser, *International Textile Design*, London, Laurence King, 1995
James Stockton, *The Designers Guide to Color*, Melbourne, Angus & Robertson, 1984
Joyce Storey, *Manual of Dyes and Fabrics*, London, Thames & Hudson, 1992
—, *Manual of Textile Printing*, London, Thames & Hudson, 1977
Various authors, *Colour*, London, Marshall Editions Ltd, 1980
Kate Wells, *Fabric Dyeing & Printing*, London, Conran Octopus, 1997
*View on Colour* magazine published biannually
*International Textiles* magazine
*Textile View* magazine

**Chapter VII**
Janet Boyes, *Essential Fashion Design: Illustration Theme Boards, Body Coverings, Projects, Portfolios*, London, Batsford, 1997
Linda Tain, *Portfolio Presentation for Fashion Designers*, New York, Fairchild Publications, 1998
For job advertisements see *Fashion Weekly*, *Drapers Record*, the *Evening Standard* and the *Guardian*
See also job agencies and other bodies listed below who help to promote young designers.

# Useful addresses in the UK

**British Fashion Council (BFC)**
5 Portland Place
London W1N 3AA
Tel: +44 (0)20 7636 7788
The BFC supports British fashion designers and manufacturers, especially with export enterprises. It encourages new talent through annual awards to students, for example the Innovative Pattern Cutting Award and for Graduate Fashion Week presentations. Under the same organizational umbrella there are a number of industry bodies including:

**British Knitting and Clothing Export Council (BKCEC)**
5 Portland Place
London W1N 3AA
Tel: +44 (0)20 7637 5577
Fax: +44 (0)20 7636 7515

**Business Technology Support Centre**
London College of Fashion
100 Curtain Road
London EC2A 3AE
Tel: +44 (0)20 7514 7526/7536

**CAPITB Trust**
5 Portland Place
London W1N 3AA
Tel: +44 (0)20 7636 3173
Fax: +44 (0)20 7636 3174
www.capitbtrust.org.uk
The National Training Organization for the British Apparel and Leathergoods Manufacturing Industry which publishes a directory, *The Graduate Post*, to help manufacturers find student graduates.

**Crafts Council**
44a Pentonville Road
London N1 9BY
Tel: +44 (0)20 7278 7700
www.craftscouncil.org.uk
Besides having an excellent contemporary gallery and crafts bookshop, the Crafts Council offers many services, such as a reference library, advice and development grants and publishes a magazine to promote crafts.

**Department of Trade and Industry (DTI) Clothing, Textiles and Footwear Unit**
1 Victoria Street
London SW1H 0ET
Tel: +44 (0)20 7215 5000
A government department that advises UK businesses on legal issues; also a fount of information concerning export regulations.

**Fashion Awareness Direct (FAD)**
42 Woodlands Road
Surbiton
Surrey KT6 6PY
Tel: +44 (0)207 792 0256
Fax: +44 (0)207 792 0256
www.fad.org.uk
An organization committed to helping young designers succeed in their careers by bringing students and professionals together at introductory events.

**London Enterprise Agency (LEntA)**
4 Snow Hill
London EC1A 2BS
Tel: +44 (0)20 7236 3000
Fax: +44 (0)20 7329 0226
e-mail: lenta.ventures@lentA.co.uk
A consortium of companies and the Corporation of London dedicated to developing small businesses, education projects and giving financial advice.

**Nottinghamshire and Derbyshire Clothing and Textile Association Ltd (NADCAT)**
Ashfield Business Centre
The Idlewells
Sutton in Ashfield
Nottinghamshire NG17 1BP
Tel: +44 (0)1623 440 612
Fax: +44 (0)1623 442102
www.nadcat.co.uk
A support centre for Midlands' business and start-up help.

**Portobello Business Centre**
2 Acklam Road
London W10 5QZ
Tel: +44 (0)20 7460 5050
Fax: +44 (0)20 8968 3660
www.pbc.co.uk
The Portobello Business Centre offers an advisory service and DTI training classes in fashion management to those wishing to set up a fashion business in West London.

**Prince's Youth Business Trust (PYBT)**
18 Park Square East
London NW1 4LH
Tel: +44 (0)20 7543 1234
Fax: +44 (0)20 7543 1200
www.princes-trust.org.uk
The Prince's Trust gives business advice and professional support as well as awarding funding for young and unemployed people planning to set up a potentially successful new idea in business.

**Register of Apparel and Textile Designers**
5 Portland Place
London W1N 3AA
Tel: +44 (0)20 7637 5577

**Shell Livewire**
Shell UK Limited
Community Investment Department
Shell-Mex House
The Strand
London WC2R ODX
Freephone: +44 (0)800 010 100
www.shell-livewire.org
Competitive awards scheme, advice and training on business startups for young people.

# Useful addresses in the USA

**American Wool Council**
50 Rockefeller Plaza, Suite 830
New York, NY 10020
Tel: +1 212 245 6710

**Color Association of the United States (CAUS)**
315 West 39th Street, Studio 507
New York, NY 10018
Tel: +1 212 947 7774
Fax: +1 212 594 6987
www.colorassociation.com

**Cottonworks fabric library**
Cotton Incorporated
488 Madison Avenue
New York, NY 10022
Tel: +1 212 413 8300
www.cottoninc.com

**Council for American Fashion**
1710 Broadway, 5th Floor
New York, NY 10019
Tel: +1 212 265 7000 ext. 522
Fax: +1 212 489 6062

**E. I. DuPont de Nemours**
1251 Avenue of the Americas
New York, NY 10020

**Fashion Centre Information Kiosk**
Corner of 39th and Seventh Avenue
New York, NY 10018
Tel: +1 212 398 7943
Fax: +1 212 398 7945

**Knitted Textile Association**
386 Park Avenue South, Suite 901
New York, NY 10016
Tel: +1 212 689 3807
Fax: +1 212 889 6160

**Mademoiselle** (fabric library)
350 Madison Avenue
New York, NY 10017
Tel: +1 212 880 8800
Fax: +1 212 880 8248

**Money in the Bank**
121 Madison Avenue
New York, NY 10016
Tel: +1 212 683 7418

**National Art Education Association**
1916 Association Drive
Reston, VA 20191–1590
www.naea-reston.org
Tel: +1 703 860 8000
Fax: +1 703 860 2960

**New York Fashion Council**
153 East 87th Street
New York, NY 10128
Tel: +1 212 289 0420
Fax: +1 212 289 5917

**Pantone Color Institute**
590 Commerce Boulevard
Carlstadt, NJ 07072
Tel: +1 201 935 5500
Fax: +1 201 935 3338
www.pantone.com

**Small Business Association**
26 Federal Plaza Suite 3100
New York, NY 10278
Tel: +1 212 264 4354
Fax: +1 212 264 4963
www.sba.gov

**The Fashion Service (TFS)**
1412 Broadway, Suite 1410
New York, NY 10018
Tel: +1 212 704 0035

**Vogue** (fabric library)
350 Madison Avenue
New York, NY 10017

**The Woolmark Company**
330 Madison Avenue, 19th floor
New York, NY 10017
Tel: +1 212 986 6222

**Fabric and resources**
Two major directories are used to resource fabrics, trimmings and supplies:
*Fashiondex*
*The TIP Resource Guide*

**Fashion trade publications**
*Womens Wear Daily (WWD)*
*W*
*Tobe Report*
*Fashion Reporter*
*California Apparel News*
*Daily News Record (DNR)*

# Index

Numbers in **bold** are illustrations

## Picture sources & credits

Peter Anderson 21; 22.
Courtesy of Helen Baker 58.
Lynette Cook 71, 72, 77, 81, 84.
Nicholas Darrieulat 138 (bottom).
Yvonne Deacon 59–61, 66–7, 69 (bottom); 85–6, 120.
Carrie Donovan 70.
Courtesy of East Central Studios 102–4; 106; 110.
Courtesy of Eastman Staples Ltd 114 (top), 115.
David Edelstein 125 (top), 126 (bottom), 127, 128 (top left).
Tim Griffiths 23; 64; 139 (top); 145 (top right); 160 (top left); 178–181.
Ian Hessenberg 121 all except top left.
Sue Jenkyn Jones 25; 40; 46 (top left and top right); 49; 50 Courtesy of Gotham Angels; 51–3; 68 (top); 73; 95; 99 (top); 104–5; 112; 116–17, 118 (bottom), 121 (top left); 124 (bottom right); 126 (top); 131 (right); 134–6; 139 (bottom); 140–1; 142 (bottom left and bottom right); 145 (bottom right); 146 (left); 148; 152–3; 156; 160 (centre); 162 (top left and bottom left); 163–5; 168–171; 173–5.
Courtesy Trevor Jones, Department of Textiles, UMIST 97.
Hannah Jordan 124 (left and top right).
Courtesy of Learning Resources at the London Institute and London College of Fashion Study Collection 17 (bottom); 18 (centre); 24; 41; 46 (bottom) 113; 114; 118 (top); 122; 128–9; 133.
Jieun Lee 65; 68 (bottom).
Garth Lewis & Ferdy Carabott, Chromafile 90–1.
Niall McInerney 1; 6–8; 10; 11; 13; 62–3 (all but top); 78–9; 82–3; 89; 92–3; 99 (middle); 100–1; 105 (bottom left and bottom right); 107; 109; 123; 131 (left); 132 (right); 142 (top left and top right); 143–4; 145 (left); 146 (right); 147; 149; 150–1; 155; 160; 166–7; 182.
Nazanin Matin 176.
Courtesy of Mattel 138 (top).
Christopher New 40 (top); 45; 46 (top centre); Courtesy of Crombie Ltd.
Ilaria Perra 74, 119.
Courtesy of Popperfoto 17 (top); 18 (top left and right); 19 (right); 20; 26; 27.
Courtesy Adel Rootstein Ltd 62 (top).
Honey Salvadori Cover.
Teerabul Songvich 125 (bottom); 132 (left); 153 (left).
Greg Stogdon 16.
Joanna Sykes 42–4.
Riccardo Tisci 152, 154.
Mark Tynan, photo courtesy Charlie Allen 130; 99 (bottom).
Malin Vester 14.
Andrew Watson 162 (right); 164 (bottom).
Naoko Yokoyama 69 (top).

## Acknowledgements

With heartfelt thanks to the students and fellow staff, past and present, who have inspired the writing of this guide through their design work, comments and contributions. In particular, thanks to Dani Salvadori of Central Saint Martins College of Art & Design for her support and guidance; to Andrew Haslam and Phil Baines for allowing me to lean on them at various stages and benefit from their experience in the field. To Roger Sears, Jo Lightfoot and Robbie Mahoney who were encouraging and instructive in the preparation of this book, and Christopher Wilson and numerous other unseen hands who helped to structure the text and layout. Special mention must be made of Cleia Smith, my editor at Laurence King, without whose patient coaxing this book would not be in your hands.

To all those whom I consulted and who gave generously of their time and experience, especially my colleagues at Central Saint Martins: Dean of Fashion and Textiles Jane Rapley, Willie Walters, Howard Tanguy, Christopher New, Nathalie Gibson, Toni Tester, Caroline Evans, Malcolm Cocks, Garth Lewis, Leni Bjerg, Jacob Hillel, Shookoh Hakimi, Christine Koussetari and London Institute archivists Steven Bateman at Central Saint Martins and Katherine Baird at the London College of Fashion.

To Tyrone Messiah who pulled strings to get my computer fixed pronto when it went down mid-project. To Celia Barnett who helped me with the mysteries of picture research and to Sally J.J. Callendar who helped coordinate visits to studios and colleges in the USA. To Timothy M. Gunn, Associate Dean at Parsons School of Design, New York and the museum and Gladys Marcus Library at the Fashion Institute of Technology, New York.

To numerous companies and individuals in the fashion industry who are supportive to education; many of whom allowed me behind the scenes, in particular: Shelley Fox, Joe Casely-Hayford, Sonja Nuttall, Suzanne Clements, Anne-Louise Roswald, Sandy MacLennan and Hilary Scarlett at East Central Studios, Alison Lloyd, Tim Williams, Andrew Tucker, Crombie Ltd, Dawn Stubbs at John Smedley Ltd, Catherine Lover, Deanne Morgan Wallace and Monica Fernandes, Adel Rootstein Ltd, Eastman Staples Ltd and the British Fashion Council.

To photographers Niall McInerney, Tim Griffiths and Andrew Watson. To illustrators Yvonne Deacon, David Edelstein, Lynette Cook and Ilaria Perra.

To contributors and designers whose work appears within: Tariq Ali, Jeremy Au Yong, Wayne Aveline, Karen Bagge, Carrie Barber, Daniel Barry, Christine Bertelsen, Alex Bircken, Peter Cash, Hussein Chalayan, Tania Chuck, Carrie Donovan, Mark Durno, Talei Fawcett, John Galliano, Dean Gardner, Connie Groh, Andrew Groves, Luc Goidadin, Sarah Heard, Jenna Highman, Henry Hilsky, Lisa Hjelm, Kimino Honma, Lutz Huelle, Nak Hyun Kim, Henrietta Jander, Anthony Keegan, Kenichi, Marie Langlois, Jieun Lee, Susanne Lieb Jason Lim, Richard Lo, Stella McCartney, Diane Mainstone, Fumie Majekodunmi, Jason Masterson-Copley, Carlos Marcant-Filho, Danny Margolin, Nazanin Matin, Noora Niinikoski, Pod Numbenjapol, Claire O'Connor, Rebecca Owens, Charlotte Palmer, Phillipa Reiss, Clements Ribeiro, Adam Richardson, Laure Riviere, Signe Rose, Michael Sikiakis, Teerabul Songvich, Oliver Steinhaus, Riccardo Tisci, Mariama Tushimeriwe, Malin Vester, Deanne Morgan Wallace, Charlie Watkins, Tristan Webber, Arkadius Weremczuk, Matthew Williamson, Samantha Willis, Gerard Wilson, Iris Wong, Trish Worral and Naoko Yokoyama.

And finally to my dearest friends and family who had the tolerance and wisdom to know when to distract me with coffee, chocolate and neck rubs.

## Dedication

To Grant Rogan, Oscar Jenkyn Jones and to the memory of my mother Grace Elizabeth.